Nature Speaks

Messages from the Consciousness of our World

Diana Lynn Kekule

Nature Speaks ~ A Journey to Yourself

EarthLight Creations
Depoe Bay, Oregon

Copyright © 2019 Diana Lynn Kekule
All rights reserved.

Nature Speaks is a work of nonfiction.
No characters have been invented; no events fabricated.
It is intended to be a loving and poetic Nature Preserve.

Published by EarthLight Creations, Depoe Bay, Oregon
Editorial: Catherine J. Rourke, The Editorial Intuitive
Book and Cover Design: Dianne Leonetti-Rux, DzinerGraphics.com
Proofreader: Suzann Panek Robins

Copyright 2019. All rights reserved. This publication may not be reproduced, distributed, or transmitted in any form by any means, in whole or in part, without written permission from the publisher, except by a reviewer who may quote brief passages in a review, and certain uses permitted by copyright law; nor may any part of this book be reproduced, stored in a retrieval system, or transmitted in any form or by any means, electronic, mechanical, photocopying, recording, or other, without written permission from the publisher. For permission requests, contact the publisher, EarthLight Creations, at *https://luvsea33.wixsite.com/earthlight,* or Facebook at *EarthLight.*

Fair Use Waiver- *Nature Speaks* claims the following Fair Use allowance of copyrighted material for quotes, poetry, and book excerpts. Pursuant to 17 U.S. Code § 107, certain uses of copyrighted material "for purposes such as...comment...or teaching is not an infringement of copyright." Quoting a short passage for illustration or clarification of the author's observations would be deemed acceptable. Similarly, a use that benefits the public, that lends to education, or is used for a "transformative" purpose also would be deemed acceptable. The genre, purpose, and character of *Nature Speaks* in the use of copyrighted work is not to copy verbatim but intended to help create something new in the reinforcement of its principles of serving life. Selected copyright material credits are attributed in footnotes throughout the publication.

ISBN #978-1-7331798-0-5
Library of Congress Control Number: 2019907644

Kekule, Diana—Nature Speaks ~ Messages from the Consciousness of our World. 1. Nature 2. Earth. 3. Consciousness. 4. Spirituality. 5. Conduct of Life.

Look through the eyes of Nature
And you shall see your Greatest Self

Acknowledgments

To Doug Bastron, a dear soul with whom I shared many days exploring nature's infinite beauty.

Heart love to dear friend, Jill Hardin, who graciously assisted in the final review of *Nature Speaks*. Her love and devotion to nature blessed this book beyond words. She sweetly supported my story from the beginning, and continues to encourage its sharing.

Appreciation to Catherine Rourke—friend, editor, and cheerleader. From our first connection regarding *Nature Speaks,* she held the highest belief and support of its message. Catherine maintained a comprehensive resonance of purpose during the course of the journey, embracing nature's voice.

Gracious thanks to Diane Leonetti-Rux of D'ziner Graphics, designer extraordinaire! Her beautiful work and unique style added a magickal touch to the creation of *Nature Speaks*. The nature beings give it an enthusiastic thumbs-and wings-up!

Many thanks to proofreader Suzann Panek Robins who assisted in aligning the clarity and purpose of *Nature Speaks*. Thank you for your cheers of praise!

Heartfelt gratitude to my Master Gnome who guided me every step in the manifestation of this book. Without his kind and persistent promptings, I would not have had the vision and courage to fulfill its fruition.

Loving blessings to all the sparkling, joyous nature spirits who jumped and giggled their way into my heart with sweet encouragement.

Humble respect to four elemental beings who offered love and wisdom to walk the journey and teach me still: The element of air, who oversees the flight of this work; the element of earth, who helped me stay grounded during the creation of *Nature Speaks*; the element of water, who reminded me to lighten up and let it flow for clear vision; and the element of fire, who keeps love's passion burning.

Much appreciation to all the internet sources of reference while researching Passage Two narratives. They provided a wealth of information that allowed me to study and express through my own words the language of *Nature Speaks*.

Contents

4	Acknowledgements
11	Preface
12	Introduction

PASSAGE ONE
The Journey Begins ~ Pilgrimage to Wholeness

14	Gaia
16	The Song of the Deva
21	Separation and Unity
22	Semblance and Diversity
23	Nature Alchemy
25	The Art of Appreciation
26	The Journey as a Pilgrimage
28	Preparing for the Journey

PASSAGE TWO
The Journey ~ Communion with Nature

34	Wisdom of the Animals
36	Mountain Majesty ~ Gift of Solitude
40	Jeweled Cave ~ Gift of Inner Beauty
44	Numinous Bat ~ Gift of Initiation
48	Wolf Song ~ Gift of Communion
52	Regal Eagle ~ Gift of Vision
56	Enchanted Falls ~ Gift of Wonder
60	Sparkling Stream ~ Gift of Spontaneity
64	Bear Bed ~ Gift of Dreamtime
68	Owl Mantra ~ Gift of Mystery
72	Forest Cathedral ~ Gift of Strength
76	Miracle Moss ~ Gift of Survival
80	Furling Fern ~ Gift of Birth
84	Silent Sound ~ Gift of Inner Music
88	Fair Fawn ~ Gift of Innocence

92	Sublime Equine ~ Gift of Freedom
96	Rolling River ~ Gift of Adventure
100	Simple Stone ~ Gift of Conscious Living
104	Frog Prince ~ Gift of Transmutation
108	Turtle Time ~ Gift of Inner Clock
112	Daring Dragonfly ~ Gift of Choice
116	King Crow ~ Gift of Vigilance
120	Meandering Meadow ~ Gift of Harmony
124	Heavenly Spring ~ Gift of Expansion
128	Flora Aurora ~ Gift of Sensuality
132	Brilliant Butterfly ~ Gift of Serendipity
136	Dainty Dandelion ~ Gift of Adaptation
140	Lucky Ladybug ~ Gift of Friendship
144	Ravishing Raspberry ~ Gift of Manifestation
148	Sentient Seed ~ Gift of Legacy
152	Miracle Soil ~ Gift of Fertility
156	Worm Wizard ~ Gift of Alchemy
160	Amazing Ant ~ Gift of Ingenuity
164	Captain Quail ~ Gift of Intention
168	Gregarious Goat ~ Gift of Curiosity
172	Beautiful Bovine ~ Gift of Gentleness
176	Playful Pig ~ Gift of Affection
180	Sweet Sheep ~ Gift of Whimsy
184	Bountiful Bunny ~ Gift of Providence
188	Rousing Rooster ~ Gift of Expression
192	Garden Gate ~ Gift of Restoration
196	Healing Harvest ~ Gift of Well-Being
200	Lovely Lavender ~ Gift of Attraction
204	Sunflower Power ~ Gift of Energy
208	Honeybee Honor ~ Gift of Integrity
212	Buddha Kitty ~ Gift of Knowing Now
216	Chipmunk Patrol ~ Gift of Conservation

220	Bird Psalm ~ Gift of Hope and Glory
224	Hummer Fuchsia ~ Gift of Abundance
228	Rose Divine ~ Gift of Love
232	Sacred Prana ~ Gift of Life
236	Holy Lotus ~ Gift of Resurrection
240	Luminous Lake ~ Gift of Reflection
244	Peacock Pleasure ~ Gift of Celebration
248	Endearing Elephant ~ Gift of Compassion
252	Sage Sloth ~ Gift of Purpose
256	Ancient Iguana ~ Gift of Strategy
260	Shaman Snake ~ Gift of Liberation
264	Shifting Dunes ~ Gift of Change
268	Calming Palm ~ Gift of Flow
272	Sea Mandala ~ Gift of Unity
276	Trickster Octopus ~ Gift of Wit
280	Soaring Seagull ~ Gift of Ascension
284	Darling Dog ~ Gift of Joy
288	Peaceful Pampas ~ Gift of Grace
292	Queen Anne's Lace ~ Gift of Elegance
296	Dolphin Dance ~ Gift of Magick
300	Whale Wisdom ~ Gift of Knowledge
304	Geese Fortitude ~ Gift of Perseverance
308	Cloud Dreams ~ Gift of Inspiration
312	Celestial Snowflake ~ Gift of Diversity
316	Rain Rhythm ~ Gift of Cycles
320	Resplendent Rainbow ~ Gift of Light
324	Sovereign Sun ~ Gift of Benediction
328	Radiant Fire ~ Gift of Passion
332	Morning Glory ~ Gift of Becoming
336	Twilight Time ~ Gift of Connection
340	Eternal Eventide ~ Gift of Peace
344	Miraculous Moonglow ~ Gift of Illumination
348	Earth Blessing ~ Gift of Devotion
352	Drum Chant ~ Gift of Spirit Dance
356	Human-Kind ~ Gift of Heart

PASSAGE THREE
The Journey Never Ends ~ Life Everlasting

- 362   EarthLight's Healing Power
- 363   EarthLight Stewardship
- 364   Life's Saving Grace
- 365   Epilogue
- 366   Nature Beings Index
- 369   Nature's Gifts Index
- 372   Inspirational Quotes and Poetry
- 380   Inspirational Books
- 382   Inspirational Videos
- 385   About the Author

Dedication

Nature Speaks is dedicated to our great Mother Earth. She is our teacher, provider, and loving parent. We reside on her sacred ground to grow into love. She is life's graceful, sublime embodiment of fertile sweetness and nourishment. Mother Earth has ceaselessly nourished my soul with wisdom, compassion, and joy. I am blessed beyond belief to share my heart with hers.

On the human side, I dedicate this work to my beloved daughter, Becca Bastron, a dear child of nature who has always been a beautiful light in my life.

This book is also lovingly dedicated to all the nature spirits, the soul of Gaia. They are the intelligent and inspiring life-force consciousness who dwell in the land of infinite creation with purity, beauty, and joy. Their precious essence enfolds us with the truth of harmony in unity.

They gently nudged, firmly guided, and unexpectedly pushed me off the lounge chair of life to crack open my heart and mind to the whispered stirrings of communion with their kingdom. Their profound messages have transcended my life into a far richer experience than I could have imagined. I am humbly forever in their debt. But they smile at this statement because *we dwell together as one!*

Preface

Nature is alive and talking to us.
This is not a metaphor.

Terrance McKenna

Dear Readers,

It is my profound joy to share *Nature Speaks* with you. It has been a blessed experience working with the beings of the Nature Kingdom in the creation of this work. It is their wish, and mine, that it enriches and illuminates your life.

In 2009 I experienced a transcendent encounter that forever changed me. The realm of Gaia opened before me as an intimate and intelligent being. I felt far from ready for any such contact, but Mother Nature's embrace had other ideas.

Over the years, after accepting this communication as part of my life, I realized the messages that the nature spirits lovingly shared were not just for my ears. They were messages of a sometimes subtle, yet profound impact to be shared with others.

In the following pages, you will hear the heart of nature speak with love, joy, and wisdom. But most of all, the illuminating message Gaia wants to impart is one of *unity*. We are all connected through the very fiber of our being. *There is no separation of Spirit.*

And so, dear readers, it is our hope that a soul remembrance be rekindled as you read their powerful words of truth in unity, where we truly are whole.

Bright Blessings,

Diana Lynn Kekule
Oregon Pacific Coast
April 2019

Introduction

A word about the Journey...

Nature's gifts resonate with each other within the infinite tapestry of life, vibrating together in the eternal stream of perfect balance. Gaia, if left alone, would indeed sustain and flourish in and of herself. Nature is one with divine harmony.

Certain words and terms, such as *magick* and *aether*, are spelled differently than standard Oxford English. I have used an archaic version to notate a particular esoteric meaning. There are also versions of words that have been capitalized to denote a higher spiritual vision.

Passage Two
Note that the eighty-one beings in Passage Two are not presented in alphabetical sequence but in order of how and where they dwell.

Narrative Introduction
A narrative precedes each Spirit Power Message. It is written by envisioning the highest light upon each being. Many creatures are abused and dwell in depressed and tormented environs. The narratives do not portray those whose spirits have been violated. The consciousness of the beings I connect with is the collective soul of that species who dwells within the pure light of love consciousness. Thus, this introduction portrays all sentient beings as whole, loved, and honored—indeed, the way life intends.

"Totem"
The word "totem" represents the sacred spirit of a specific animal, plant, mineral, or element. The spirit of this being dwells in the highest state of consciousness; thus, through its example, it offers humanity a heightened vision for living.

Spirit Power Message
This is the channeled communication I received from the nature beings' essence energy. It is a unique part of them, through their voice, sharing what would be beneficial for humanity to hear. I am deeply honored for simply serving as a bridge for the intelligence of Gaia to speak to and through. You, as the reader, are also able to be of the same consciousness to receive their words of wisdom, love, and joy. It requires only an openness of heart and vision to be infused with their guidance toward living within the harmony of one.

Dream Song
Dream Song is my deep prayer of thanksgiving to each nature spirit who bestowed their divine consciousness upon my soul and to all life. After embracing the simple yet powerful message from each being, I felt an overwhelming sense of gratitude for their beautiful energy. The term "Dream Song" reflects my heart-prayer invocation of ongoing connection to their life-affirming gifts. It is my hope that you be filled with the same openness of gratitude and cultivate consciousness to connect with them in daily life. I am in great humility, on my knees, in profound gratitude. My heart is full in the fountain of their blessing. May you also be infused with their loving spirit.

"Human-Kind"
The last chapter of Passage Two is called "Human-Kind" instead of Humankind. It is written this way to emphasize that humanity possesses an inherent kindness within. Lest we forget, our highest self is innately kind and compassionate.

Gaia

There is in all visible things an invisible fecundity...a hidden wholeness. This mysterious Unity and Integrity is Wisdom, the Mother of all, *Natura Naturans.* There is in all things an inexhaustible sweetness and purity, a silence that is a fount of action and joy. It rises up in wordless gentleness and flows out to me from the unseen roots of all created being, welcoming me tenderly, saluting me with indescribable humility. This is at once my own being, my own nature, and the Gift of my Creator's Thought and Art within me, speaking as Hagia Sophia, speaking as my sister, Wisdom. I am awakened, I am born again at the voice of this my Sister, sent to me from the depths of the divine fecundity.[1]

"Hagia Sophia"
Thomas Merton

---

[1] *Emblems of a Season of Fury,* copyright ©1963 by The Abbey of Gethsemani. Reprinted by permission of New Directions Publishing Corp.

Passage One

THE JOURNEY BEGINS
Pilgrimage to Wholeness

In the Beginning—the story of...

The Song of the Deva

What suddenly and profoundly changed my life happened one beautiful spring afternoon in 2009.

Resting in the tranquility of my backyard garden on a cool March afternoon, I relaxed in a heavenly haven of flowers, trees, and sky. A graceful flowing pond and caressing breeze soothed me as I closed my eyes in sweet repose. I was at peace with the world. Reclining on a chaise lounge, I breathed deeply, inhaling the pure air filled with golden sunlight and fragrant evergreens.

Suddenly, a flock of crows flew overhead, cawing loud and steady. I awoke out of my reverie. They sounded persistent, and I mused that they were heralding a proclamation. Just as quickly, dozens of songbirds encircled me in the trees chanting in a concert of breathtaking song. In disbelief, I looked around and listened intently to this sublime symphony.

I felt embraced by a powerful vibration in the atmosphere, as my awareness began to perceive a very lucid, elevated realm of dynamic tingling energy. The birds continued to sing and caw steadily in unison above me.

Unexpectedly, I heard a feminine voice from within and around me. It permeated the garden. It spoke from the sky, the birds, the trees, the bees, *from me*—from everything and everywhere. I sat frozen, trying to comprehend the source. The voice said: "We have come to you through birdsong, because of your love and attraction to it."

Instantly my whole being perceived the presence to be a Nature Deva, an over-lighting being who guides the creation and protection of the natural world.

"The source of nature needs to be revealed to mankind," she declared. "We are telling you of the importance of communication with nature, because your destiny is in jeopardy."

Breathing slow and deep, I sat still, listening. I felt suspended in a timeless energy existing in an infinite space. The encounter was surreal like a dream, but the most lucid and sublime ever experienced. Everything felt ethereal—harmonious and full of grace. I sensed I had entered an elevated realm of consciousness governed by pure love, with a blessed benevolent energy surrounding me. It was a transcendent moment in eternity.

Then, suddenly, the birds stopped singing as mysteriously as they began. Slowly opening my eyes, I breathed deeply and looked around the garden, filled with wonder. I looked up to the heavens with a prayer of hope for humanity. A profound peace enfolded me.

The next morning while in bed, words flooded my consciousness. It was the Deva. She emphasized a yearning of nature for unity with humanity. I began writing her message, which she said all nature vibrates:

By faith, we call unto you to blend with our forces.
Reach for the highest, in union with Divine Nature.
We come within you to raise our energies
In hope for your harmony with earth
Because life as you know it is in your hands.
Look to your very thoughts
In the workings of the mind of man
And seek the element of Peace in all that you do.
To raise to this consciousness
You must stand on the Throne of Love.
We are working with your spirit-soul to do so
But the word must come from you in agreement.
Nature, through the heart of Spirit, is offered to you.
Be pleased with her life, and enjoin in prayer:
Prayer for Peace, Prayer for Beauty, Prayer for Harmony.
She offers these to you at all times, in love.
See yourself as part of the natural life ~
Your body and soul are made from
The same source as Nature:
Herein lies your connection ~ the source of One.
Praise is unto you from Heaven on Earth
As you raise your thoughts on high to Peace.
Our voice is within every mountaintop, every grain of sand
Every breeze in the sky, every flame of the sun
Every raindrop of dew, every flower petal glistening
Every butterfly rising, every wolf echoing.
We are Life, and you walk within our Kingdom.
Praise our life as gifted, and blessed unto you.

What a beautiful universal message—full of hope, beauty, and love for humanity. This holy prayer, this communion with the Deva and emergence with Gaia, filled me with a profound humility and devotion for all life. Knowing the important role nature plays in the survival of life on earth became a crystal clear, urgent message.

Deep within, I knew love and honor for the realm of nature was vital for humanity to survive. This came from a place of inner feeling and ancient knowledge. I remembered the powerful words of one of our greatest contemporary humanitarians, Albert Schweitzer, who prophesied, "Until he extends his circle of compassion to all living things, man will not himself find peace."

Together, one by one, we can raise our beautiful selves and give the love we truly are to the glory of life. Within our most cherished hearts, all humanity desires to dwell in peace and joy. Through harmony with the Kingdom of Nature, we can transform ourselves to fulfill this dream by recognizing our divine selves, where Spirit resides and dwells in love.

We are surrounded by beautiful beings everywhere. We are blessed beyond belief. The animals, plants, minerals, and elements have great gifts to share. These gifts are intricately interwoven within us through one fabric of life. Spirit is alive and well in all beings—from the great planetary orbs in the heavens to microscopic atoms pulsating in a grain of sand. We share the embodiment of Divinity within—the source of creation, our authentic essence.

After these experiences, my senses slowly began to open to the heart of Gaia. I felt I was led on a journey through a series of revelations gracefully intertwined with her soul—an emergence with the infinite realm of wondrous gifts she lovingly bestows. And, as I discovered her precious gifts, I came to realize their essence mirrored the greater self of humanity.

Subtle encounters with the consciousness of the natural world became heart-opening communions. I began, spontaneously and intuitively, to *hear* inspirational messages emanating from its intelligence and instinctively realized they were treasured gifts for humanity.

For several days afterward, the Deva encounter moved into a mist. For over a year after the experience, I questioned my sanity. What had I really seen? What had I really heard? Was my mind overflowing with the wildest of imaginings?

I kept to myself. In profound contemplation, I reflected the implications: I could be viewed as living in non-reality, the victim of delusional rantings—a crazy woman! It sounded like the stuff of madness, but it truly was a gladness Either way, I had been *out of my mind.*

Ultimately, one thing could not be denied. What I experienced was beautiful. It was heart-opening. It was love. How could that be false? The voice and the message were from a source of pure love.

In the deepest recesses of my being, I knew love was truth. All the profound beautiful teachings from mystics, masters, teachers, and sages throughout time could be summed up in one word:

LOVE

Love and do what you will.

St. Augustine

Separation and Unity

Universal Connection

In God's wildness lies the hope of the world.
When we try to pick out anything by itself,
we find it hitched to everything else in the Universe.

John Muir

All life is infused with an indwelling spark of life. This has been termed as God, Spirit, Divinity, Universal Life Force Energy, Infinite Source, etc.

Life originates from and is a form of this consciousness. Creation births from this state of being. This energy dwells within everything, from a miniscule grain of sand to the blazing sun—nothing exists without it. A rock may appear to be lifeless, but within it is teeming with dancing atoms.

We are a cherished part of nature. Often what is missing from our lives is a true sense of relationship to the world around us. The magick of the natural world opens a path to harmony with the consciousness of all things. Most of us have experienced moments of this in the realm of nature. This union can feel astounding or subtle, but always heart-opening.

Within Gaia's kingdom you can be discovered anew, over and over. As you regain a sense of place in the cosmos, this relationship can bring peace, belonging, and joy. It is an opening of perception that expands the heart and mind through the truth of awareness.

Semblance and Diversity

Unique Beauty

*There are only two ways to live your life.
One is as though nothing is a miracle.
The other is as though everything is a miracle.*

Albert Einstein

Mother Nature is infinitely intricate and divinely diverse. The brilliant patterns of creation are as endless as the universe eternally expanding. We are blessed with the opportunity to experience this miraculous, unfolding panorama of life. A blade of grass, a busy ant, a soaring sparrow, a rocky shore—all sing the song of diversity.

Consciousness is vibrant. Take a moment to see the phenomena of life all around. We live in a sumptuous world filled with a wealth of beauty. I call this expression of infinite consciousness *miraculous!*

Life springs forth from this energy, and nature guides the creation of design, color, form, and texture. We are all part of this creative pulse of life. It is our source of oneness from whence we are born and evolve. And from this cosmic heart-seed, life grows with exquisite uniqueness—miraculous, indeed.

Nature Alchemy

A Journey to Yourself

Science cannot solve the ultimate mystery of nature. And that is because, in the last analysis, we ourselves are part of the mystery that we are trying to solve.

Max Planck

Alchemy is described in *Webster's Dictionary* as "an apparently magical power." Since ancient times, alchemy has been recognized as a magickal process of transformation and creation, symbolically turning base dross into brilliant gold.

"Magick" in the context of occultist Aleister Crowley's philosophy, is a term used to show and differentiate the occult from performance magic and the movement of natural (but little understood) energies from the human body and from natural sources to manifest change, i.e., "the Science and Art of causing Change to occur in conformity with Will."[2]

Nature beings are the life essences in all that we see, hear, taste, smell, and feel in our natural world—the animal, plant, mineral, and elemental (earth, air, water, and fire) kingdoms. We are all connected by the element of matter, as well as consciousness.

The life purpose of earth spirits is to assist in the creation of beauty and its inherent companion, joy, in the natural world. In divine alchemy, each being's virtues and characteristics mirror humanity's true essence in our highest state. This is the fabric of the oneness of all life. As we remember this, there is no separation in communion with life.

---
[2] Crowley, Aleister. Magick, Book 4.

It is Gaia's heart-desire to be one with humanity in all things as we dwell upon Mother Earth together. Harmony is the core of this work. The Kingdom of Nature bids us closer in this deep connection of self, mutually moving with love.

What I have been asked is to listen and share the nature spirits' inspiring messages. Filled with transcending insight and embracing love for the merging of our hearts and souls, they invite humanity to join in sacred stewardship of life.

Mother Nature is one of our greatest teachers and allies. Each being, from a titan star to a tiny ant, is infused with a unique gift to life. Each helps humanity discover a path to wholeness in the joyous spirit of one.

Our world offers the great gift of living in well-being. An absolute stream of well-being eternally flows to and through life. Each of us has the choice to dwell there or not. Gaia's words of wisdom and encouragement can help guide us to our natural state of being within this divine flow. It is the art of living that they speak.

I define this as nature alchemy, because being in alignment with this flow is a transformation of self and all life—for we are united in sentient Life-Force Energy.

Conscious communion is at hand. Join with your nature-kin as you journey through this kingdom within and around you. It is ever-filled with sublime beauty, love, and joy.

The Art of Appreciation

Gaia's Blessing

Nature's beauty is a gift that cultivates appreciation and gratitude.

Louie Schwartzberg

Here we go, into the Land of the Brave!

How courageous it is to put aside one's personal trials and see nature as an affirmation to living. Cultivating appreciation is one of the greatest services to life, for it radiates outward. Gratitude it is a beacon which will alight any road. And Gaia's beauty can light the way.

A dewy flower, a darting dragonfly, a shimmering crystal, a billowy cloud—our world invites an opening to gratefulness. Trusting the unfoldment of life through the eyes of our world is a guiding and healing balm toward well-being. As our eyes open to the splendor of this realm, we see natural miracles all around. Nature flows with the innate rhythms of life and bids us to join in the journey.

The art of appreciation grows from trust. When one trusts the flow of life, it opens doors for the manifestation of infinite possibility. Trust is an invitation to universal energies to come hither and initiate divine intervention for resolution. Aspiring to gratitude as a life practice can enhance every aspect of living. It assists in the dissolution of fear—the culprit of unhappiness. Let Gaia guide you through her beauty.

The Journey as a Pilgrimage

Gift to Self ~ An Inspired Life

*My church is not found in any building
for all things are sacred and the earth is my altar.*

StarShine Surreal

In philosophical terms, pilgrimage is described as the course of life. It is also the journey of a pilgrim who travels to a shrine or holy place as a devotee.

Nature Speaks embraces both aspects of the pilgrimage. It offers the gift of awakening to creation as a sacred place—a profound temple created from the living world. When nature is revered as a sentient being, one becomes a conscious devotee with an inspired appreciation of our natural world.

As you discover nature's inherent gifts on the pilgrimage, you develop an intimate relationship. Gently flowing through the awakening process, you instinctively remember these gifts to the world are also a part of your inner being—a mirror of your own beautiful self. Then *you* become a gift to life.

Thus, your pilgrimage is an odyssey of self-discovery through the miraculous world of creation. Every living being reminds you of the spiritual consciousness residing in all things—including yourself. By the power and virtue found in nature, you can find the strength and dignity to become your greater self. And in the sharing of this self, you help to change the journey of the world.

The path of the pilgrim is beautifully described by Tanis Helliwel, founder of the International Institute for Transformation, in this passage:

"Ultimately, the goal of pilgrimage is to arrive at our heart's centre. What do we find there and how do we interpret the answers? This answer may be profound, life-changing and so dramatic that we can no longer return to the life we led. The answer might as easily be a simple knowing that a mother's kiss, a sunset, a playful puppy is as important as a vision of Christ. Whatever the answer, we need to fully embrace and assimilate the inner and outer journey, while at the same time realizing that the pilgrimage never ends and reveals itself at different stages of our life. It is not the destination so much as the focus of the journey that defines the pilgrim. Pilgrimage sums up all life's experience—that which can be understood and that which cannot." [3]

Blessed Be

---

[3]   *Pilgrimage with the Leprechauns,* Blue Dolphin Publishing, 1997

Preparing for the Journey

Guided Journey Primer

There is healing in the trees for tired minds and for our overburdened spirits, there is strength in the hills, if only we will lift up our eyes. Remember that nature is your great restorer.

Calvin Coolidge

Below are suggestions for a beneficial experience on your journey of intimate, natural heart-communion. The nature beings who dwell within and around our world—the animals, plants, minerals, and elements—want to communicate with us in loving partnership.

I can't share this enough: *nature is one of our greatest teachers and allies.* There are infinite inherent benefits of communicating through the process of listening to our natural world. In communication with these spirit-beings of Mother Earth, you can receive compelling messages on how to live within your natural state of well-being, which is peace with yourself. Peace with yourself is harmony with life.

Nature journeys center on active participation and an opening of heart and mind. This is how to commune with nature. It is a proactive vision quest of energetic connection with the nature beings, our endearing next-of-kin.

One does not need be present with their spirit to bond. Energetic relationship is a reality. If you are unable to be in the same physicality as a being you wish to commune with, envisioning is a viable tool. Looking at an image of the earth being can help with this process.

There are four stages to enhance the flow of union: Relaxation, Infusion, Imagination, and Communion.

RELAXATION

The first step is conscious breathing. Slow and deep, at your own comfortable pace. This is a purification process of breathing clearing energy into your body.

Prana is Sanskrit for breath—the life-giving force. Imagine light-filled Prana entering your body, touching every cell with its healing essence. As you inhale, allow Prana to flow to and through you. As you exhale, imagine stress and discomfort leaving your body. During this experience, you may even feel a tingling sensation, as you are filling your body with the pure energy of Source-Love.

Relaxation is the process of allowing yourself—body, heart, and mind—to LET GO! Letting go of what may be gripping or demanding attention at the moment. These three aspects can be challenging. It takes a conscious act of giving yourself permission to put any demands of the body, heart, and mind on hold for the time being, as you allow yourself to become open to a new experience of high spiritual vibration and connection. It is the act of *being here now*. This is the mindful intent of the journey—to release the ties that bind.

To soothe bodily discomfort, locate and visualize gentle contentment. It is important for the body to be as comfortable as possible, to aspire to release physical shackles.

If the heart emotions are currently causing stress, practice consciously comforting yourself with the anticipation of an intimate bond with Gaia's beautiful spirit. This can override high emotions and may even diffuse them after the journey.

The use of the mind is vital for this practice, and it is beneficial to calm overactive thought processes. As we hold the world's demands within, we block our prospects of spiritual connection to that which heals. Mindfulness can offer a clearing space for forward movement into the realm of restoration.

Not only do these practices benefit life as a whole, but they also have the innate power to open doors of perception of the healing power of nature.

INFUSION

After you have integrated a gentle state of restful awareness—a great gift to yourself—a natural opening occurs. It is a blossoming of soul-space. Herein, a state of natural harmony takes precedence. You are in the receiving state of grace. This is a letting go and permission of self for union with divine synchronicity and serendipity. A feeling of peace may be powerful at this stage, softening into a quiet space. You are now in the seed-stage of communion—a most fertile place of manifestation.

IMAGINATION

"Imagination is more important than knowledge", intuited Albert Einstein. This is where your spiritual abundance begins growing. Imagination is your divine inheritance, a gift into worlds unknown. It is a powerful tool that can guide you into the transformation of self. Imagination can touch the heavenly realms—a portal into worlds within and without. This is where you allow your psychic senses to take you on spirit journeys of awakening. Whatever surfaces as a comfortable feeling is from Source energy. It is a safe place to explore and discover, to grow and embrace yourself and the beauty of life. Nothing has ever been created in the physical before it has been imagined. This is the fertile space where inter-consciousness communion takes place beyond the physical realm.

COMMUNION

Now you are on your way! Engaging relaxation, infusion, and imagination are doorways to heart-based relationship with Spirit. We dwell in the same etheric space as nature beings. They are a breath away. They long for a sharing of beauty, joy, and harmony with humanity. As you enter into this realm, the field is wide open for a vision quest and a sacred melding of heart. You will be practicing the wise and ancient indigenous ways of Earth Whisperer. You will be guided toward powerful communion with the beautiful beings of our world whom we dwell with every day, in every way.

JOURNEY ON
Go as far as you want with each being through the passage. You may want to just absorb the message of one at a time, or you may resonate with several in a wondrous stream of nature consciousness. Just enjoy the journey.

*The Source of nature
needs to be revealed to mankind.
We are telling you of the importance
of communication with nature.*

Song of the Deva

Passage Two

THE JOURNEY
Communion with Nature

Wisdom of the Animals

The Shape of Story

In every culture throughout the world, there is a rich vein of animal myths and stories that are related to the primal beginnings of the world. These cycles of stories are often the very first stories ever told. In them, the wisdom and lore of the first animal beings relate how human beings should behave, revealing how things were first instituted. We see such animal story cycles from the unbroken oral traditions that pass through the classical, medieval and renaissance times from the fables of Aesop to the animal stories of Rudyard Kipling's Jungle Book and Just Ho stories. Buddha used the Jataka animal tales to teach people about right behaviour. In these stories, it is the animals that are in charge.

The animals of such stories are not domesticated, tamed or subdued to the will of humans, nor are they anthropomorphized animals or storybook characters whose actions mimic humans. They are wise beings in their own rights whose words and actions cause the world to come into being. They are almighty, omniscient, and full of wisdom. Some are tricksters like Coyote or Raven, who both involve themselves in the laying down of laws for humans and whose lateral thinking discovers useful tools for living such as fire or agriculture. They are guardians for those times when humans overstep the respectful mark whereby all living creatures can be threatened by destruction or they are animals who partake in humanity in some way, like the Centaurs who are teachers of humanity, bringing music, art and other essential skills.

We live in a time where me most urgently need the wisdom of the animals and creating creatures. Although Darwinian theories of evolution have told us that human beings are the summit of the evolutionary ladder, at the top of the food chain, we need the salutary wisdom of the animals to put us in our place, to remind us too that we are animals – sometimes animals of "little brain". And like that supremely humble anthropomorphism Winnie the Pooh, a bear of little brain, with a little help from our animal advisors, we can sort out even the most troubling of problems.[4]

The Element Encyclopedia of Magical Creatures
John and Caitlin Matthews

---

[4] Sterling Publishing, 2005

Mountain Majesty

Gift of Solitude

> *Solitude gives birth to the original in us to beauty unfamiliar.*
>
> Thomas Mann

Mountain's magnificent presence has existed before time immemorial. We look upon Mountain Majesty with awe, and its holy face has been the glorified object of countless artists' inspiration. Since humans first discovered Mountain's power, we have sought it out to traverse its rocky path as a pilgrimage for the soul.

Throughout the ages, humanity has pondered Mountain's significance in the realm of the absolute—feeling its elevation above earth higher and closer to infinite Spirit. With reverence in our heart, we know Mountain, reaching up to the heavens as a beacon of the eternal.

Mountain emanates an immense aura of power from its constant being. It is a celestial monument ascending to the heavens though the parting clouds, radiating its essence throughout the cosmos. Standing tall above earth on the highest peak, Mountain Majesty rises as a towering temple of the sublime.

Here, it is still and serene. The sound of peace prevails. There is naught except the profound silence of Spirit. It is the sound of exaltation. Here, on top of the world, between heaven and earth, rests the Divine. The radiant magnitude of this holy place emanates through life in an endless horizon of Mountain's spirit.

Mountain Spirit Power Message

My power rests within you, as we are One.
You carry my strength within
For we are bound together by stone and bone.
As you look to your heart, do so alone
For in solitude lie doors to the unknown.
Relax in this knowing, for it is good.
Your soul can be found in the mist of quiet
As your strength of spirit dwells there.
It is by this realm that you shall find me
And know the power within.

Dream Song to Solitude

In the aura of your magnificence
O Mystic Mountain
I know that I am you!
As I touch upon the soul of your strength
Through sacred solitude
I know that I am you.
I seek you now, for this divine transformation
And I become you.
I stand tall betwixt heaven and earth
And receive your powerful blessing
For now I am whole, within your realm
O Great Mountain.
And as I descend upon the grounds of Gaia
In the Sacred Warrior stance
I lead my thoughts to the purpose of my path
And walk your trail back into my self.

Thank you, O Mountain Majesty
For your great Gift of Solitude

Jeweled Cave

Gift of Inner Beauty

> *Whole life is a search for beauty.*
> *But, when the beauty is found inside,*
> *the search ends and a beautiful journey begins.*
>
> Harshit Walia

Sheltered within the subterranean heart of Mountain lie hidden treasures to behold. Deep within the caverns, in a luminous grotto, exquisite stones of great wealth and beauty take shape. This is Jeweled Cave, a revelation of infinitely sparkling gems.

Throughout time, these beloved gifts of Gaia have been highly sought. Since the discovery of these riches, humanity has explored every corner of the world through treacherous trails, scaling massive and difficult terrain—sometimes at great peril.

The brilliance of Jeweled Cave's allure holds an historical and mythical aura of wealth and power. Within the hierarchy of royalty, gemstones have signified a high standard of rank, affluence, and influence, celebrating the one adorned. Through the emotion of love, we have bestowed jewels as symbols of affection and desire. Since ancient times, precious stones have been worn in cultural celebration and ritual throughout the world with pomp and circumstance. Mysterious Cave has fascinated scientists, artists, poets, philosophers, and musicians in a quest for the allure of inner beauty.

Jeweled Cave silently sparkles in the hidden realms yet is eternally present for the discovery of beauty. The Spirit message is clear: priceless treasures are hidden within. Seek and you shall find the unfoldment of your glorious Self.

Cave Spirit
Power Message

I sparkle in your eyes, yet it is you who shines!
Your vision of me is of yourself
For we dwell in the world of One.
My light is your light, and it shines greatly.
Come into my radiance where you can see thy Self.
And as you uncover the brilliance of your soul
It is here where I dwell
In the midst of your Holy Heart.
This is the true essence of thee
Always in the form of the Divine.
Your purpose, then, is to uncover, to excavate
Your beauty within.

Dream Song to Inner Beauty

Within your walls, O Jeweled Cave
Shines the essence of all
For I am the same as you.
My facets reflect the Divine.
Within your luminous sparkle
I see myself shining, smiling.
I am a mirror of you.
The light of your blessing humbles me
And yet, I feel the power of beauty
Shining directly from you
Through me, coursing through my veins
Alighting myself
Filling me with my own true light.
These are the jewels of my inner cave.
Radiant forever, in grateful praise of you.

Thank you, O Jeweled Cave
For your great Gift of Inner Beauty

Numinous Bat

Gift of Initiation

*I have learned things in the dark that I
could never have learned in the light, things
that have saved my life over and over again,
so that there is really only one logical conclusion.
I need darkness as much as I need light.*

Barbara Brown Taylor

Within silent Jeweled Cave, nuances of soft squeaking can be heard. It is dawn, and Numinous Bat returns to the dark roost after a night of flight. Bat possesses keen echo-location night vision through soundwaves and is the only mammal achieving sustained flight.

Numinous Bat is regarded in some cultures as a shamanic medicine totem. Bat Spirit actively journeys through the dark, to the unconscious depth of divine intuition where dreams and visions emerge. Guiding us through the twilight into worldly illusion, Bat then brings us back into the subconscious inner cave for unity and sacred introspection of truth. "Darkness and night are mothers of thought" is a Dutch Proverb that enlightens the beneficial balance of both.

Initiation births in the rich darkness. It is here where light becomes visible. Numinous Bat represents the fertile darkness, the source of personal rebirth. Each dawn it returns to the depths of Mother Earth and from the womb is reborn to emerge again at dusk. Thus, Bat's flight beckons us to journey into the transcendent riches of our emergent soul-self. Fear not, for the inner darkness births the miracle of growth.

Bat Spirit Power Message

I take you into fertile and fruitful darkness
Where initiation dwells.
I am a Spirit of the night
Opening doors of truth and insight.
In the darkness dwells the light.
I fly away from the bright of day
Where distraction pervades.
I follow the transcending Spirit path within.
I journey in flight
To the inner light.
Take time to look inside, away from the mundane.
Sacred birth is your name.
Illuminate thy Self.

Dream Song to Initiation

Great Bat, master of the unseen
Guide me within my inner domain.
As I call upon you in flight
I follow you into my sacred night.
And here I will see
Visions upon dreams of what I can be.
Initiate me!
And who I am emerges in new life
With thee.
There is a brilliance of light
Within this flight
Into the depth of the womb-like awakening night.

Thank you, O Numinous Bat
For your great Gift of Initiation

Wolf Song

Gift of Communion

*I live to hold communion with all that is divine
to feel there is a union 'twixt nature's heart and mine.*

George Linnaeus Banks

Deep within the hollowed Bat cave, a hypnotic echo of lone Wolf Song can be heard. Wolf howls to connect with others, to assemble the pack, to sound alert, and to communicate across great distances. Its song can be heard for up to a fifty-square-mile radius.

A highly intelligent and social animal, Wolf is naturally eloquent and when howling together, harmonizes with others rather than sounding the same note, thus creating the illusion of a greater number of wolves. Wolf Song includes up to twelve complementary synchronized vocal-related overtones and can remain constant or vary smoothly. The gift of communion at its sweetest!

As a result, Wolf's crooning creates an eloquent melodious chant that humans are inexplicably drawn to. Throughout time, we have intuitively raised our heads and opened our ears upon hearing its entrancing song. It is pure sound. It is the very essence of instinctual nature that is a great part of us all.

Although much misunderstood and maligned by some societies, many cultures regard Wolf as an honorable teacher and a powerful symbol of the freedom of spirit—the intrinsic essence of the soul. Thus, Wolf Song becomes an empyrean mantra in the aetheric[5] form of collective prayer—a sacred union with life.

---

5   Aether is a radiant, energetic element. It is associated with power, wisdom and clarity. http://thecbg.org/wiki/index.php?title=Elements_(Savage_Age). Aether (quintessence) is the fifth element that binds the four classical elements: water, fire, earth, and air together. It is the strongest and most powerful element in the series. *https://neptolumbia.fandom.com/wiki/Quintessence_(element).series.* According to ancient and medieval science, aether also spelled ether, is the material that fills the region of the universe above the terrestrial sphere. The concept of aether was used in several theories to explain several natural phenomena, such as the traveling of light and gravity. *George Smoot III. "Aristotle's Physics". lbl.gov. Archived from the original on 20 December 2016*

Wolf Spirit Power Message

I am Spirit of Wolf.
I call you to reach out
In communion with life.
I am the call of your soul
Yearning for sacred union.
For our songs are united as One.
They speak of the brotherhood and sisterhood
Of all beings.
Our voice is the Song of Creation
Singing through the aethers of the heavens.
Our voice—it is the call for One
In harmony with life.
Sing together with the Song of Spirit.
Let it be heard on high.

Dream Song to Communion

O Wolf Spirit, I hear you!
As your song enters my soul, I hear you.
The voice of Spirit
Flowing freely through the heavens.
And as I merge and flow with it in communion
I hear the call of One
In all beings and in all things
Flowing to and through eternal life.
I am one with its voice.
It streams through the aethers of time and space
Into my heart—forever calling
Forever free—forever me.

Thank you, O Wolf Song
For your great Gift of Communion

Regal Eagle

Gift of Vision

> *If you go as far as you can see*
> *You will see enough to go even farther.*
>
> John Wooden

In transcendent flight, Eagle sails on the wings of Wolf's mantra, rising in the heavens. Soaring in splendor, Regal Eagle loftily glides through the sky, communing with creation in a miraculous sight of true nobility.

Eagle's keen vision is one of the sharpest of all animals, and 3.6 times more powerful than humans. Thus, Regal Eagle is a master of the skies, surveying its kingdom with a razor-sharp sense of panoramic perception.

Reigning as one of the most powerful birds of prey, Eagle's supreme stature and prowess also leaves it undefeated in the animal kingdom. Weighing as much as twenty pounds with a wingspan of up to eight feet, it boldly soars above earth, displaying stunning acrobatics. It can take wing up to altitudes of 10,000 feet and achieve speeds of seventy-five-plus miles per hour in descending glides.

Regal Eagle has been revered by humankind since the beginning of time, depicted as early as the Stone Age. We have regarded Eagle with fascination, high among the towering trees, viewing its sublime flight as one of nature's wonders.

Eagle aspires us to power and inspires freedom of the soul. Its stately presence is represented as an enduring emblem of valor and supremacy in countless cultures.

Thus, the role of this magnificent bird has become an ultimate living symbol and universal portrayal of omnipotence. It is no wonder we have looked to Regal Eagle throughout history as a gift of vision—a prevailing symbol of strength, pride, and independence, instilling these very qualities within our hearts. Eagle Spirit tells us to fly high, to be the noble soul we are.

Eagle Spirit Power Message

Vision is above perception.
As you see me fly high in the sky
Come and touch my soaring Spirit.
It is here, where freedom of the soul rises
Where the true vision of life unfolds.
It is an ever-changing landscape.
Your freedom lies
In the knowing of change.
The changing perception of time in no-time.
Vision is the key
To find your place with me.

Dream Song to Vision

O Eagle, you fly to me!
Through my heart, and into my head
Your Spirit soars.
I feel one with you.
We fly into the sky
Into the sunlit horizon
Of clear vision.
We fly into the mist of the unknown
With focus and power.
Life is seen through your eyes
Within the sphere of all possibility
Where all dwell within the realm of your sight.

Thank you, O Regal Eagle
For your great Gift of Vision

Enchanted Falls

Gift of Wonder

Wonder is the beginning of wisdom.

Socrates

Below noble Eagle's flight, wondrous waters flow. Earth's life-pulse streams through Enchanted Falls. Waterfall's natural phenomenon has been viewed with wonder since we first opened our eyes to its captivating spirit. We have traveled far and wide to experience the sensation of Waterfall's effervescence, witnessing its vitality with awe.

Throughout the ages, artists and poets have adorned their work with Enchanted Falls. Landscapers and gardeners build shrines to Falls, enhancing the peace and beauty of the environment. In a world where miracles seem lacking, we flock to witness its dynamic essence. Enchanted Falls nourishes our search for the miraculous in our lives.

Feeling the heart of the Falls is an inspiration, a revitalization, and a cleansing of spirit. It feels akin to being washed anew with fresh life. With wonder-eyes, it is realized that life may indeed begin again afresh and unencumbered, like the sparkling waters reborn, coming forth, over and over. This is the miracle of Enchanted Falls.

To see Waterfall with spiritually open eyes is to be cleansed of mental and emotional debris. Enchanted Falls can rejuvenate and clarify the senses, releasing our inner spirit to experience the magickal purity of its transcendent gift of wonder. Wonder opens doors to the eternity of creation.

Waterfall Spirit Power Message

I am here, before your eyes.
Witness my beauty, my power, my joy!
I am all-encompassing and shower myself on thee
In wondrous love ~ feel, it is free.
Feel me flow within your own.
I rise up and cascade down.
I splash you and open you.
I rush to you and mist you with my power.
I am the manifestation of your free soul
In every hour.
Breathe my sparkling essence
Feel my flowing reign
As I anoint you
With the joy of wonder within.
You are a pure Child of Spirit.
Blessed are you to be thee
Let your Self flow free.

Dream Song to Wonder

O Beautiful Falls
You touch me with your sparkling heart.
I am showered by your wonder.
You feed my soul with such delight
I can barely contain my jubilation!
Such joy, such vitality.
I stand within your
Flowing heart of love.
I bless your holy being.
I adore your vibrant soul
As you come tumbling down
With love upon me.

Thank you, O Enchanted Falls
For your great Gift of Wonder

Sparkling Stream

Gift of Spontaneity

*Once we believe in ourselves, we can risk
curiosity, wonder, spontaneous delight
or any experience that reveals the human spirit.*

E. E. Cummings

As Waterfall joyfully flows, it fills the world with Stream. Stream plays an important role in the biological habitat of its surrounding areas. The vicinities of life species and riparian zones are harmoniously united by Stream through the generous wealth of its life-giving essence in the continuation of creation.

Stream Spirit conserves the primary critical core ecosystem of earth. All forms of streams—rivers, creeks, tributaries, brooks, rivulets, and runnels, are the life-blood of Gaia, flowing toward her sea-heart.

Sparkling Stream blesses us with its healing waters—offering food, shelter, and the purification of mind, body, and soul. These gifts are all spontaneous offerings from its essence of love. Stream naturally delights in caressing, skipping, tumbling, and splashing its way with joy to a spontaneous path of life-discovery.

This is the message of Sparkling Stream. It sings the heavenly song of love and joy, meandering downstream and blessing all in its path with the miraculous gift of spontaneity.

Stream Spirit Power Message

I flow into life. I flow through you.
You are in the stream of life.
As you behold my waters within your senses
Know that I call you to ride the current
Of the natural flow of things.
Do not hold back, for I call you forward.
Come with me into the world of spontaneity.
It is here where life is lived with joy
For the soul is free to move on its own.
Feel yourself at one with the whole of flow.
Allow the divine moment, let it come and go.
As I wash over you, I break a static shell
And life's energy surrounds you well.
I am the healing Waters of Life.

Dream Song to Spontaneity

I come to you with my heart, open and wide.
You bring me joy!
I feel your spontaneous flow
Wash over and shower me
With the light of your soul.
You guide me anew.
In my freedom I flow and splash and jump and skip.
Your take me to the moment and movement of myself.
And I laugh ~ I am in bliss over me.

Thank you, O Sparkling Stream
For your great Gift of Spontaneity

Bear Bed

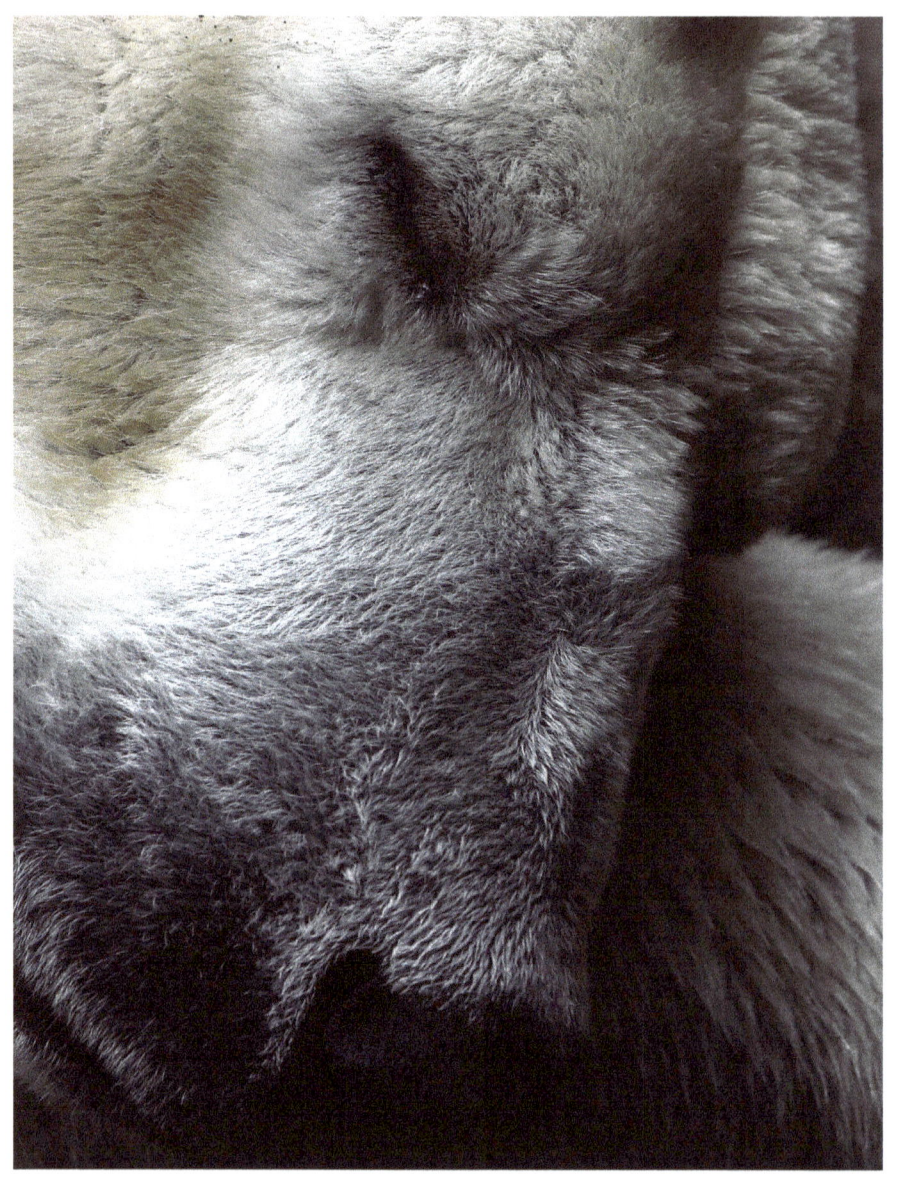

Gift of Dreamtime

Man is a genius when he is dreaming.

Akira Kurosawa

In the quiet autumn forest, great Mother Bear drinks deeply from cool, running Stream. She slowly lumbers over to her hallowed den where she will dwell in sacred hibernation—the magickal state of dreamtime.

Mother Bear dreams from October through April, avoiding the harsh deprivations of winter. In early autumn, she gathers nesting materials into a cave, burrow, rock crevice, or hollow tree to create her winter hibernation bed. Mother Bear typically builds her den just large enough to squeeze through with her cubs, who join her in deep slumber.

During dreamtime, Bear's metabolic rate drops by half. Her heat rate drops from fifty-five beats per minute to eight, and body temperature from one hundred degrees Fahrenheit to eighty-eight degrees Fahrenheit. She is in a state of suspended animation during the great sleep.

Bear Spirit is a guru of dreamtime. While Bear may drowsily awake after one hundred days to eat, drink, release body waste, or exercise, she retreats once again to her sacred bear bed to connect with Spirit through the inner journey of mystic dreamtime.

In alchemical symbology, dreamtime gestates an epiphany, a great initiation of self. Bear bed represents the physical life going inward, receiving illumination. As insight is gained within, outward growth follows.

Dreamtime is a mystery to humans, unless we also go inward. Yet it is here where great Bear totem touches the eternal, gaining the wisdom of the ages, to be reborn again in the height of spring growth.

Bear Spirit
Power Message

I am great Mother Bear
Slumbering in the bed of sacred dreamtime.
I call on you to rest your mind, your body.
Go into the silence of your inner dream lodge.
Here the fruits of your heart and soul ripen
And blossom forth into new awakenings.
I hold this space for you within dreamtime
As a link to your eternity.
For as you go within
Life opens before thee.
Follow the light of the path
And go forth.
I guide thee to the discovery and everlasting
Birth of Self.

Dream Song to Dreamtime

O Sacred Bear, I rest in you.
I feel your warmth enfold me
With the promise of new growth blossoming.
It is here where my resting soul opens.
My heart mends
And they receive the blessings of your dreamtime.
It is here where I hear the voices
Of life's spirit calling me home.
My heart rests in you, O Mother Bear.
Softly, you call me into the slumber of truth within
Sometimes hidden, but now flowing forth.
I hear you, O Power Bear
Rising up within, calling me to my true self.

Thank you, O Bear Bed
For your great Gift of Dreamtime

Owl Mantra

Gift of Mystery

> *The most beautiful experience*
> *we can have is the mysterious.*
>
> Albert Einstein

Flying over hidden Bear Bed, the distant, drifting call of Owl can be heard. Throughout history, Owl has been recognized and revered. Not only has Owl garnered respect from scientific communities, but also from ancient, indigenous, and spiritual cultures.

Owl's greatness lies not only in its distinct physical structure and heightened abilities, but also within the sublime world of magick and mystery. Owl totem is honored as possessing the sacred symbolic qualities of wisdom, intuition, power, protection, transition, mysticism, messages, and secrets.

One of Owl's most prominent features and unique characteristics is its haunting gift of voice. We can hear it in the dark quiet of the night and early morning, sounding… *whooo, whooo, whooo*. Owl's evocative song has the ability to draw us into ourselves and outward into the secrets of nature. "The real trick to life is not to be in the know, but to be in the mystery," intuits theoretical physicist Fred Alan Wolf in the cutting-edge film, *What the Bleep Do We Know?*

Owl is the enchanted primordial path to the great unknown. As we follow Owl, it instinctively leads us to an inner contemplation of Divine Mystery—that sublime, illuminating place where life gives birth unto itself.

Owl Spirit Power Message

Here, hidden in the air, in the trees, I AM.
I call you unto me.
By my voice…calling…calling.
I bid you enter into the realm of the mystic.
It is here where life knows itself
For all is revealed in the sound of the wind
And in the trees.
My mantra is magick.
I forever hold that claim
And gift you with its name.
For as you allow mystery to dwell
It will forever present be
A sign for you to see
The true beauty of thee
And the Oneness of we.

Dream Song to Mystery

O Sacred Owl, I hear you calling
Calling me.
Into the depths of myself.
It is here where the mystery unfolds.
Shining like a flame
Blooming like a flower's soft fragrance
Opening to the brightness
To the beautiful miracle within.
It is here where the mystery unfolds.
The spark of creation.
Your flame, connected to all flames
Is within all life.
Every layer upon layer
A shining grid of sparkling light.
A mystical connection.

Thank you, O Owl Mantra
For your great Gift of Mystery

Forest Cathedral

Gift of Strength

*In some mysterious way, woods have
never seemed to me to be static things.
In physical terms, I move through them;
yet in metaphysical ones,
they seem to move through me.*

John Fowles

Sage Owl echoes through Forest Cathedral, the spirit of the woodlands. Here is life's benevolent congregation of trees who unite diverse ecosystems in a cohesive, sustainable environment—a unique atmosphere dwelling harmoniously.

Forest embraces all kingdoms of life with equal devotion. The world's woodlands are vital to all life as they provide a multifaceted range of resources: carbon collection, regulating earth's climate, purifying water, conserving soil, and functioning as hydrologic flow modulators. Thus, our world's great groves of trees bestow life with some of the most essential life-sustaining elements of our biosphere.

Life and death abound within Forest Cathedral—in the Great Way. It is a holy place, shared by an infinite number of species, living and dying, moment by moment. This dynamic ecosphere cultivates and nurtures the diversity and strength of life—each element, each being, depending upon one another, nourishing in perfect balance. Here dwell the thriving ways of Spirit. The noble woodlands gently oversee and care for its family of sentient beings, blessing life in all ways.

A walk among the sacred woods yields a cleansing breath of clarity. The great groves offer the gift of strength. Standing among Forest, we can gain an immeasurable power within. And so, dear friends, go out into the Forest Cathedral, and become one with the trees—and yourself.

Forest Spirit Power Message

We are of ancient blood, born of the stars above.
The essence of our heart is nobility
As we protect and nourish the world.
You see the physical gifts that we bear
Yet displace our soul.
And in this forgetfulness, you lose our sacred contact.
What could be an awakening of Spirit
Is only a source of heat.
Come to us now with arms outstretched
And feel our gracious hearts together
Beat as one.
For we are givers of life
And you, a holy receiver.
It is through this gift that we were born.
And when you give us love, we bear it mightily
For it flows within our veins to bless all others.
Everything thrives stronger
Through the gentleness of love.
Then you are a giver of life.

Dream Song to Strength

O Sacred Forest, I feel your strength!
I am always held in your loving arms
And feel you embrace my soul.
I feel your power course through my veins.
It is a bold, yet gentle force
And holds the power of the universe.
It is the strength of my path
The strength of my truth
The strength of my vision.
I stand tall to be the One I am
And you are here and show the way.
It is here where I grow.
In the presence of your sacred being
Rising to the heavens, I am One with you.
I am blessed and healed
In the cathedral of your love.
My soul exalts in abundant blessings
Of your noble power growing strong within.

Thank you, O Forest Cathedral
For your great Gift of Strength

Miracle Moss

Gift of Survival

Survival is nothing more than recovery.

Dianne Feinstein

Throughout the great Forest dwells a most simple and elegant being—Moss. Miracle Moss is one of the most resilient and versatile plants in the world, requiring no cultivation and growing in light intensities too low for other green plants to survive. It grows in every habitat from deserts to streams, from the Arctic to the Antarctic.

A master of suspended animation, when dried even for years, Moss can revive itself with just a mist of water, springing back to vibrant life again. Benefitting life on earth, it removes pollutants such as ammonia and nitrates from the atmosphere, synthesizing them for its own means.

It is quite amazing to think of this glorious spongy, hummocky, emerald-green beauty as a genius of survival. Considered to be simple in evolutionary terms, there is a great lesson from this rootless, almost cell-less plant—that of subsistence, the continuation of life.

We do not have to be super-humans to survive. "It is not the strongest of the species that survives, nor the most intelligent, but rather the one most adaptable to change," notes Charles Darwin. Moss Spirit's message is one of survival using our own unique gifts of being, through the nourishment of them. Honor your gracious gifts, recognize the wonder of existence through them, and they will serve you and life well.

Moss Spirit Power Message

I am a master
A master of life.
Yet I am simple-dwelling
Living without strife.
I survive through my own means
And behold, great beauty from me streams.
I hug earth in such a way
That I add beauty
And life to my day.
I am Miraculous Moss
And show you the way
To be a simple power
In the beauty of yourself.
Allow that to grow
And bless your day.

Dream Song to Survival

O Sweet Moss!
I see your loveliness all around
And know it is simple
Yet so profound.
You do not ask for accolades
Nor recognition in any way
But simply in your survival
Do you bless my day.
My gifts do I honor
In the continuation of being
For they have their own reward
In the blessed survival of life.

Thank you, O Miracle Moss
For your great Gift of Survival

Furling Fern

Gift of Birth

> *I had seen birth and death*
> *but had thought they were different.*
>
> T. S. Eliot

Around the globe, flourishing Moss and Fern thrive abundantly together. Ferns grows within a wide variety of habitats—from remote mountain heights to arid desert rock crevices, from wetland environs to sweeping meadows.

As an ancient plant, Fern is older than dinosaurs. It was thriving on earth 200 million years before the first flowering plants evolved. What can be said about Furling Fern is that it enthusiastically survives through the mystery of birth and death.

During the Victorian era, when flower symbology was a popular passion through the beloved *language of flowers* trend, Fern was regarded as possessing magickal qualities, and its motif was ardently replicated in many forms.

In esoteric terms, the visual wonder of viewing the birth of Fern fronds from fiddleheads can imbue a spiritual sense of the miraculous. Curling upwards from a tight feathered spiral, the fiddlehead truly expresses the profound act of birth in all life.

Let us marvel at this mysterious beauty of perfection, for we are, in the deepest sense, eternally birthing ourselves with the one energy of Furling Fern.

Fern Spirit Power Message

We abound earth with feathers, wings, and light.
Ho, we give birth to you!
With our curling and furling delight
We show you the birth of self within
Ever outward.
Watch our soft form take shape
Before your very eyes
And know that we are one with you.
For our Spirit, and yearning for life
Grows strong within you too.

Dream Song to Birth

O Holy Fern, I see my birth in you.
As your curling fronds gently open to life
I become one with thee.
I am your Spirit manifesting
Your new birth gracing me.
As we spring forth eternally anew
We become Source together, it's true.
From this blossoming forth of Spirit within
I join creation in celebration again.

Thank you, O Furling Fern
For your great Gift of Birth

Silent Sound

Gift of Inner Music

*See how Nature—trees, flowers, grass—
grows in silence; see the stars, the moon,
and the sun, how they move in silence.
We need silence to be able to touch souls.*

Mother Teresa

Flourishing Fern grows in the depths of Silent Sound through the natural flow of inner music. Silent Sound is in harmony with the mystical Music of the Spheres, an ancient philosophical concept regarding movement of the celestial bodies as a form of music. All nature hears and moves in this way, flowing with the heavenly heartbeat of life.

Inner music is a movement, a fountain of sound heard within. Listen with your deep interior senses. It is a harmonic convergence with the vitality of creation—the Life-Force Energy.

Inner music can be heard… as the dolphin flies through the waves, when the perfumed rose shimmers in the morning dew, when the newborn sea turtle opens its eyes, when cavern crystals sparkle in a soundless cave, when towering trees pray in heaven's gaze… it can be heard. This is the miracle of inner music—Silent Sound singing through the breath of life.

"Silence is the fullness, not emptiness; it is not absence, but the awareness of a presence." John Chryssavgis' beautiful quote conveys the exquisite connection to creation that we all innately possess. There is fragrant, divine music amidst the silence of self in the conscious listening of inner music.

Silent Sound Spirit Power Message

Inside me
All life dwells.
Into my mystic space
This divine place
Surrounds you, and you dwell.
I am the spark of creation
The eternity of Self.
I am teeming with life
In the celestial symphony.
Know the mystery of
Inner Music
Is the song of the soul
Where you always will dwell.
Rest in this knowing
For all is well.

Dream Song Inner Music

O My Soul!
I hear your song of eternity.
You are within
Singing all sounds.
Into the silence of Self
I hear our masterpiece
Chanting in the heavens.
Our hymn to life
The birdsong of love
Within and without
Forever singing.
And I am at peace
In the celestial harmony.

Thank you, O Silent Sound
For your great Gift to Inner Music

Fair Fawn

Gift of Innocence

*Innocence and unconditional love are one.
Innocence is starting from the beginning,
opening up to all there is.*

Kwan Yin

Within Silent Sound, gentle Fawn walks and grazes, the epitome of grace and innocence. Many of us stop in our tracks with quiet respect and admire Fair Fawn's delicate countenance.

Throughout history, Fawn has been portrayed in poetry, music, and folklore, and is revered as a genteel animal of great sensitivity and intuition. Fair Fawn is honored as being acutely perceptive with its keen sense of rooting out abundant wild herbs. Ancestral Native American and Celtic peoples would follow Fawn to retrieve medicinal herbs beneficial for healing.

As we look to Fair Fawn for guidance, we can understand that innocence is the peaceful purity of the true self coming forth. When we gaze upon its inner and outer beauty, we are transfixed because Fawn is symbolic of our own soul.

Poet John Updike intuited, "The essential self is innocent, and when it tastes its own innocence knows that it lives forever." Bringing the beautiful essence of Fair Fawn into our hearts can help us realize our gentle, loving sweetness within and connect with the true heart of our soul. This exalted awareness leads to the realization that all life is born of innocence. Dwelling within the innermost core, virtue is intrinsically present.

Fawn Spirit Power Message

The softness that I bring you
Has yet to be discovered.
It is softness rounded at the corners
An innocence of mind and spirit.
You are this very soul.
I place this softness upon your breast
Hoping you will feel it and do the rest.
As you become your innocent self
You are the heart of who you truly are
In all ways, the purest sense of gentle love.
Go now and be this.
Your beautiful true Self.
Strength lies within your innocence.

Dream Song to Innocence

O Dear Fawn
I see my purity in you.
As I go my way, I can find you
In me, within me.
You touch that place in my heart
Where it is sweet and free
Where nothing has been put asunder.
I go my way with you
And am free to be the soft strength of me.
Your embracing, loving eyes are filled with me
And our precious heart is one.

Thank you, O Fair Fawn
For your great Gift of Innocence

Sublime Equine

Gift of Freedom

> *I have seen things so beautiful*
> *they have brought tears to my eyes.*
> *Yet none of them can match the gracefulness*
> *and beauty of a horse running free.*
>
> Anonymous

As gentle Fawn rests with inner grace, another being takes charge that heeds attention. Here stands the quintessential power and stance of Sublime Equine.

In ancient cultures, Horse was viewed as a glorious carrier of the gods, pulling chariots of deities into the heavens on celestial journeys and battles. Unicorns were adored pets and confidants of the divinities. Wise winged Pegasus rode through the clouds in epic flights that man could only dream of.

Throughout history, Sublime Equine has been symbolic of the highest forces of power and freedom. The magnificent steed has been portrayed in the arts as a great creature of these two aspiring qualities—physical and spiritual strength.

In the wild, Equine runs free in great herds with heart-pounding speed and grandeur. Native Americans intuitively knew the grounding power of Equine who was connected to the spirit of the wind. Among all the totem animals, it is Sublime Equine who portrays the strongest driving force of universal freedom.

Even through domestication, Equine maintains a strong energy and drive of its own. This Power Animal gives us pause in the wake of realizing the vital importance and expression of our own personal freedom.

Equine Spirit Power Message

I am the Power of Freedom
Run with me!
Your soul dwells here within infinite realms of reality.
For in your power, you are a force
Of Spirit running with me.
We run together and create Divine Energy.
We create worlds.
Do not lose sight of freedom, it is your right.
Your absolute Self, a gift to life.
Strive to stand in this supreme state of being
With freedom ever-present.
It is your great growth, a gift from me.
It will serve you well.

Dream Song to Freedom

O My Soul, freedom of my soul
How you have yearned to follow and grow.
I now listen to you inside.
Deep within where you always speak to me
I will follow thee.
O Great Equine, you lead the way
Your force of energy guiding my day.
You are truly Spirit moving me
To the power within.

Thank you, O Sublime Equine
For your great Gift of Freedom

Rolling River

Gift of Discovery

> *No man ever steps in the same river twice*
> *for it's not the same river, and he's not the same man.*
>
> Heraclitus

Mighty Equine stops to take refreshment at River's flowing, nourishing body. Rolling River speaks of all the travels through the millennia of time—by all humanity, and creatures of life. It shows us visions of discoveries and adventures unfolding, its course flowing through eons of time. You can see the history of the world through this great water of life. This is the heart of Rolling River.

It is the soul of discovery, where the joy of encountering adventure resides. River flows eternally, sometimes gently, sometimes rushing. Within its kingdom, one can realize the possibility of adventure is always present—here in this great River Spirit of life. It speaks to us of these things.

Mankind has traversed River seeking new experience through diversity, sometimes through treacherous waters, and sometimes lazily sauntering along. But it does not take the physical act of travel to enjoy the gift of discovery—rather, simply an awareness of our inner and outer senses offering the exquisite exploration of life. Sometimes delicate and subtle, sometimes surging and bold, but always potential discovery.

Rolling River tells us to embrace the journey of life, for just around the proverbial corner can be another adventure to embrace, another escapade to partake.

River Spirit
Power Message

I am here… at your feet!
I take you to places known and unknown
Within and without.
For the adventures of life abound
In all directions… flowing, flowing.
From where you stand
From where you start
It is always a beginning.
And I flow through you.
Come with me on this journey of Self.
Explore, voyage, vision quest
Follow your own gift of discovery.
Dwell within this revelation
In the ever-adventure of life.
It is your soul's right.
Joy of discovery is the key
To find you and me!

Dream Song to Discovery

O Rolling River
Magnificent being!
I flow with and through you
Amidst this moment of eternity.
You offer the world of adventure
Everywhere—inner and outer.
Always flowing, always free
this world of discovery.
Of myself and others
And into life's sea of mystery.
Always for me to feel, grow, and be.

Thank you, O Rolling River
For your great Gift of Discovery

Simple Stone

Gift of Conscious Living

The unexamined life is not worth living.

Socrates

In the body and fields of great River lies Simple Stone. Stone is a grounding force of physical life. Its solid mass is a building block of manifested physical construction.

Man has learned to use Simple Stone in the creation of dwelling places—from humble homes to massive cathedrals of light. Stone—grounding, strong, and solid—is a structure from whence we may receive a feeling of safety and security, protected from the elements.

Since time began, Stone has held a wide, yet subtle attraction of its inherent qualities, drawing us to its inner life. As an outwardly passive being, its essence is one of simple conscious living. Stone serves all who seek to use it respectfully.

Conscious Living is the heart-act of being in a state of simple presence and present to serve. It is a way of walking, taking one intentional step at a time in stewardship with life. In this way, Simple Stone guides us to the harmonious balance of all things.

Conscious Living is the building block to transformation toward unity. This state of being is not merely existence, but a fullness of Spirit. Life opens with a clear vision of purpose. It is a sharing of the dream with all beings, and a remembrance of our birthright—the sacred marriage of life with itself. Simple Stone is mindful of the dream and shows us the way to live it effortlessly.

Stone Spirit Power Message

I am the Rock of Life.
All things come unto me.
For I am the binding force of creativity.
Here on earth, you will see
That we come together to be.
In this mutual space we share living
For our paths cross and we stand as one.
Walk on me and know my strength.
It is good and grounding
For your intentions and interactions.
Keep your living heart-solid and strong
And here your path will move along.
Conscious living flowing to and through
I am always together with you.

Dream Song to Conscious Living

Great Stone, I am at your feet.
I honor your strength which my heart does seek.
We share the living dream
Of conscious power.
For you are the namesake in every hour.
Power Stone
You show the way
To stand, to walk in consciousness
Grounded day by day.
I hold your sweet simplicity and know
This is the heart-way to grow.

Thank you, O Simple Stone
For your great Gift of Conscious Living

Frog Prince

Gift of Transmutation

*In Nature, there is less death and destruction
than death and transmutation.*

Edwin Way Teale

Perched on mighty Stone along the river bank, Frog Prince speaks! Here sits an intimate family of toads atop a rocky stand looking curiously like a noble throne. Frog sings with great gusto, loud and deep—belching and croaking, bobbing up and down. This royal symphony of baritones fetches a laugh!

But there is a mystical secret about Frog Prince. By the subtle power of Spirit—through its voice—Frog transmutes negative energies surrounding Mother Earth, diffusing them into the aethers[6]. What princely power, what a royal gift! This is Frog's sacred role, its divine path. Frog Prince sings a love mantra.

Listen deeply to Frog's passionate voice. Within its song is an ancient alchemical process of transmutation. With divine assistance from Frog Prince, Gaia absorbs toxic energies from life, transmuting and expelling them with deep love to do no harm. A mystical purifying and balancing vitality is bestowed.

Like all Nature, this is a metamorphosis of Spirit. Frog Prince shows us that we can take what is heavy and negative within and transmute it into the lightness of love. This is freedom of the soul. This is what the mystics referred to as "turning dross into gold."

---

6   Refer to footnote on page 49.

Frog Spirit Power Message

I am the Voice of Transmutation.
I connect with the forces of life, all around.
Dwelling deep within sacred Mother Earth
You can hear the sound.
This mixture of energies is absorbed
Through alchemical creation.
Transmutation is my game.
I assist in the balance of harmony.
Through my voice, I sing out negative forces
To disperse and dissolve.
To do no harm.
You may join in this venture
It is your right.
Diffuse the negative, wherever you may see
And bridge the gap between you and me.

Dream Song to Transmutation

O my Frog Prince
May I never forget you!
You, who are the restorer of life.
You, who are the great balancer.
Take me by the hand and lead me
To those places of change within
That must be forged.
Lest I die an inhibited soul!
You sing the song of Spirit revived
By your magick I survive.
Sometimes swift, sometimes slow, I must go
To this sacred place of reformation
Through my cycle of growth.

Thank you, O Frog Prince
For your great Gift of Transmutation

Turtle Time

Gift of Inner Clock

*Time is a very healing place,
one in which you can grow.*

Denise Tanner

Great Turtle walks with a slow beat through Frog's powerful song. Ancient Turtle has walked the earth for 220 million years. It lumbers along betwixt land and water, steadily following its course, slowly but surely. There is no hesitation, only an innate focus of intent. Turtle looks ahead with vision and purpose. It is a powerful creature of these two worlds, and a master of both—in its own Turtle Time.

Not only is Turtle an environmental master, but also an adept of the mental and physical planes, with a mind sharp with fortitude. Turtle totem is a genius as it follows its inner clock of calculated physical movement with mental clarity. Turtle Spirit shows the path ahead. Moving together brings us to our own tempo, at our own stride, without limitation from others.

A state of being to be reckoned with, Turtle Time is the knowing of self. Our inner clock is a personal source of higher direction, progressing at a pace in perfect movement, in any given moment. Upon the road of life, heed Turtle in unity with the effort of intent. Follow your own journey.

Turtle Spirit Power Message

I walk the line of committed purpose.
Nary does my step subside.
For I am the Great Path
The inner clock of no time.
It is your time, your pace
It always comes back to you.
Listen… step by step
The only journey you will need
Is your inner clock for you to heed.
Remember this path to your Self.

Dream Song to Inner Clock

Ancient One, you move, tried and true.
I endeavor to be one with you!
Turtle Time leads the way
And here my heart aspires to stay
In line with inner time.
For me to remember this
I must move and pace
Within and without my life space.
The gift of inner intent
Will be my grace.

Thank you, O Turtle Time
For the great Gift of Inner Clock

Daring Dragonfly

Gift of Choice

When a great moment knocks on the door of your life, it is often no louder than the beating of your heart.

Boris Pasternak

As ageless Turtle treads the terrain and swims flowing waters, luminous Dragonfly swirls in the air. Iridescent wings move its lithe body—blithely hovering one moment, then swiftly darting another. Daring Dragonfly knows the moment of opportunity and choice.

An ancient being of 300 million years, Dragonfly can fly up, down, backward, and sideways—displaying a master craft of flight. As one watches in wonder, miraculous Dragonfly displays stunning aerodynamics.

Daring Dragonfly demonstrates the freedom of flight inherent within. Its sky-dance reminds us that a choice of opportunity and movement abounds—the magickal stuff of flowing life.

Watching Dragonfly shimmer as it flashes and dances in the air can bring a sense of inner joy and outer sparkle. Its energetic frolicking reminds us to be bold enough to embrace a sense of choice in life, which can open doors to the source within—the desires of self.

An amazing fact about Daring Dragonfly is that it lives only about one year. In its precious time, this radiant being dwells in the high-spirited land of vitality. Don't deny yourself the bliss—fly high and thrive! *Carpe Diem ~ Seize the Day!*

Dragonfly Spirit Power Message

As you see me fly
There are no boundaries
No limits, no borders in the sky.
This is my message to you:
Your opportunity of flight is boundless
Your soul is free!
Choose what is best for thee.
This can be your driving force from within
Your sense of direction, you see.
As you fly toward a new choice
Remember your sparkle as you go
For this is truly who you are, as well you know!
Let yourself be free and fly with me.

Dream Song to Choice

O Dragonfly
You are my wings!
I take flight with you.
I see my opportunities
And know all they need is me.
There's this one, and that one
Whether I go, or stay, it is wise to see
It is truly only up to me.
My choices come from within.
My soul has called them forth
So I can decide to go any way on course.
Ho! The ones I choose will soar with me!

Thank You, O Daring Dragonfly
For your great Gift of Choice

King Crow

Gift of Vigilance

Eternal vigilance is the price of eternal development.

Gordon B. Hinckley

Where radiant Dragonfly thrives in the sky, so too does King Crow make its stance. How many times have we heard Crow caw loudly in proclamation of attention? "Be vigilant," Crow commands. "Take notice!" Flying high, the great black bird descends onto thick, lofty branches rustling in the trees, or straddles post and wire with the same message: discern.

In Native American legend and myth, Crow was believed to have the power to speak and therefore considered to be one of the wisest birds, associated with the great mysteries of life.

Bold Crow stands with sovereignty. King Crow is the ancient Bird totem of alchemical mysticism. It declares and shares a companion call to all who listen. Crow speaks of the hidden teachings of wisdom through the conscious act of awareness. It speaks of the constant vigilance of the Sacred Warrior on the path. Crow holds the space of attention for the inner and outer worlds, bringing transcendence of heart through the flight of life.

King Crow proclaims vigilance in each moment, in each movement. Following the heart is the way of the conscious warrior. This is the true spirit of kings and queens!

Crow Spirit Power Message

As you attend to the inner and outer
There are signposts at hand.
Spirit speaks!
Much will be uncovered
By your watchful vigilance.
Take notice through discernment
And eternally move from a place of balance
Within these two worlds.
Pettiness is not for you!
The openness of Spirit
Is a watchful path
Flowing in all directions.
Make your move and post your mark
With a Sacred Warrior's heart.
Blessed are you, O Kings and Queens!

Dream Song to Vigilance

King Crow, I fly to you!
I aspire to fly with you
In your direction of mindfulness.
For my sacred flight in life
Is at attention and ascension with you.
Let me forever keep in vigil this devotion
As I walk my earthly path.
Let me enfold it under my wings
And know what steps to heed
As I follow my heart through life
Let it be one consciousness, indeed!

Thank you, O King Crow
For your great Gift of Vigilance

Meandering Meadow

Gift of Harmony

Little things seem nothing, but they give peace, like those meadow flowers which individually seem odorless but all together perfume the air.

Georges Bernanos

Crow flies far and wide and enjoys the sweetness of Meandering Meadow. Beautiful Meadow is of vast ecological importance because as an open, sunny space, it attracts and supports flora and fauna who could not survive in other conditions. Meandering Meadow bestows harmony to life.

Countless species flourish in the bountiful fields of Meadow. The six main animal classes of insect, bird, mammal, amphibian, reptile, and fish all enjoy its benefits. Vibrant Meadow is a haven for life, a nourishing being bestowing the fragrance of love. Shelter, food, and comfort dwell here. Harmony of life abides.

As an intimate and cherished part of nature, so we too may also partake in sweet Meadow's gift of harmony. Senses become calm and balanced within its fields of tranquility. Meandering Meadow speaks through a lovely unity of diversity, flowing effortlessly in wave upon wave of beauty and peace.

Meadow is life's vale where inherent harmony perpetually dwells. The divine balance of all elements blends in perfection. All diversity is hailed as nurturing and unifying to each other—the sacredness of life. In Meadow's natural state, harmony eternally manifests.

Meadow Spirit Power Message

As you rest within my world
I embrace your soul with serenity
In the quintessence of a natural life.
Above, beneath, and within all that you perceive
Your divine inheritance is to feel this freely.
The illusions of unrest that you feel
Move anxiously against thee.
Raise yourself higher, rest within
The infinite fountain of your deepest wellspring.
For within my Spirit of harmony
You will find yourself in me.
I am the life your soul seeks.

Dream Song to Harmony

As I walk through enchanted sweet Meadow
My soul cries out in delight!
For I am brought to this heavenly place to remember
The genuine, the unchanging
The stream of well-being.
The flowering of harmony is
Forever flowing within all.
I am at peace.
Life flows through an agreement of unity
Whether I remember or not.
And here, I unfold into perfection.

Thank you, O Meandering Meadow
For your great Gift of Harmony

Heavenly Spring

Gift of Expansion

Spring is nature's way of saying, "Let's party!"

Robin Williams

Beautiful Meadow bursts alive come Spring! Heavenly Spring is the annual fruition from the inner withdrawal of rest to plant seeds for growth. Life develops this phase of evolution to expand!

Expansion is the blossoming forth of inner life into outward experience—a culmination of all that has been gestating through patience and the miraculous. Heavenly Spring is Mother Nature's way of reminding us of the presence of flowering eternity. What may look stagnant or inactive is just life's growth in embryonic state. The seed is very much alive and growing, as are all beings.

Within earth life, evolution of self takes both time and love. It is a natural process of becoming anew. And wherever that process takes place is where one will expand and bloom. Through expansion, one's life may flourish into experiences not yet encountered. These experiences then offer self-reflection within, and so the cycle continues, *ad infinitum*—life!

Heavenly Spring proclaims, "now is the time to manifest, and relish, what has been cultivated within." Beautiful Spring is the mirror of inner wonder. The blooming of self is a limitless experience. One may choose many ways to feel expansion. Choose wisely for well-being.

Spring Spirit Power Message

I am that which is you!
We expand together.
I am a reflection of you
As you flower your life.
I grow and blossom into exquisite beauty of Self.
Through time I am infinite
And as you blossom, so must I.
We are connected by forces of creation
In the ever-expansion of eternity.
Go now and grow!

Dream Song to Expansion

O Sacred Spring!
I am dazed by your beauty.
How can you be a mirror of me?
Am I of such splendor?
Why, yes, you say
We are one in every single way!
I will heart-cherish this
O blessed Spring
And bring beauty to your name.
I will aspire to live in your light
Of eternal growth.

Thank you, O Heavenly Spring
For your great Gift of Expansion

Flora Aurora

Gift of Sensuality

The spiritualization of sensuality is called love.

Friedrich Nietzsche

In the glorious heart of Spring, exquisite beauty of color, form, and fragrance overflow. One's senses may wantonly ascend into the heightened sense of sweet sensuality of Flora.

Ecstasy abounds in the light of jubilant Flora Aurora. Bobbing their lively radiant faces, Flora smiles at the sky in celebration of life. The richness and profusion of blooming Flora bursts into creative expression. Sparkling rainbow colors surge forth in infinite form with heady scents of Mother Nature's beautiful body. Sensuality is a living presence here.

What does this mean? That life is to be enjoyed, by all our senses. Divine nature lusts for life. And existence on Gaia will grow richer in the sharing of her sweet delights. Flora enhances the appreciation of our senses.

Humanity has attempted to dissect and disrespect sacred sensuality. The pleasure and passion of love and joy is at the heart of beautiful, creative pleasure. Flora Aurora lovingly presents, through the delight of Mother Earth, the gift of sensuality for our senses to feast upon.

Nature invites us every moment to touch, smell, and feel her sensual being. She expresses her bounty, grace, and splendor through the exquisite manifestation of life in glorious creation. May we know and be blessed by her love.

Flora Spirit
Power Message

O Sweet Soul, come, enjoy our song.
We sing to the glory of living!
We are that which induces the senses
To the spirit of joy.
Surround your world with our song.
We praise all sensuality
With blessings from our heart.
Enjoy the bounty of our joy
And it returns to you one-hundred-fold.
For within your senses is the gift of the Divine.
Each time you enjoy the purity of your senses
You delight in the mind of creation.
For that which pleases you, pleases life
For we are all together.

Dream Song to Sensuality

O Flora Aurora
I am bewitched by your charms!
You lead me into the field of bliss
As I inhale your loveliness.
I bow before your heavenly beauty
And incomparable sensuality.
You are a being of sweet expression
Of all the delights of the world
To be infused, breathed, and enfolded into.
Rapture is your name
Allure is your game
As you offer to me
Sacred Sensuality.

Thank you, O Flora Aurora
For your great Gift of Sensuality

Brilliant Butterfly

Gift of Serendipity

Serendipity is the faculty of finding things we did not know we were looking for.

Glauco Ortolano

Into the fields of luscious Flora shines Brilliant Butterfly! As this delicate creature flies from flower to flower drinking sweet nectar, serendipity is perceived.

As a result of drinking nectar, Butterfly collects and spreads pollen, multiplying life! Little Butterfly is a master at creating new growth of fruits, vegetables, and flowers, thus helping to produce a healthy environment. Such synchronicity!

From our view, serendipity is an unexpected surprise, a happy happenstance. It is a magickal event, one which universal consciousness has synchronistically orchestrated for a beneficial purpose. Little do we know what surprises are peeking around the corner!

Like gentle Butterfly, many acts of kindness have a hidden element of serendipity. Actions have a way of drifting from one to another, in an expansion of manifestation. Butterfly totem shows us the natural beauty of grace and the beneficial results of living in that state.

Ethereal Butterfly expresses the sweet serendipity of magickal moments as it flutters around in the garden. We delight in this beautiful being because of its lovely aura, and when it comes near, we are enchanted. So is the destiny of Brilliant Butterfly!

Butterfly Spirit Power Message

I shine in your light!
My magick is in you, as you see your own.
I dance in the sweet nectar of life.
Come join me
As I spread joy and feed the world!
It is an ever-expanding state of being.
We flutter together on earth
Sharing our gifts through the joy
Of giving and receiving.
As you spread your wings, so you invite life to join.
And what could be more serendipitous
Than a dance of sweet celebration?
Come fly with me
Let us beautify others with their own sweetness.
O Blessed Be!

Dream Song to Serendipity

O Beautiful Butterfly
You shine light on me.
Come and dance with me!
Your charming presence is a delight to my soul.
I glimpse your heavenly beauty
As you bless those you touch
And invite your sweet nectar within.
It is the bliss of serendipity!
What magick do you behold?
For it is a flutter in a moment
Where a glimmer of joy can unfold.

Thank you, O Brilliant Butterfly
For your great Gift of Serendipity

Dainty Dandelion

Gift of Adaptation

> *Adaptation is a profound process.*
> *Means you figured how to thrive in the world.*
>
> Charlie Kaufman, *Adaptation*

Little Butterfly flutters as nature bursts with hearts of Dandelion! This petite and tender flower is queen of adaptation! Dainty Dandelion may be found within cracks of cement and asphalt, within the rockiest of crags, and thriving in dry dirt. This golden flower glows and flourishes amongst the toughest of life's challenges.

Little unassuming Dandelion is a totem of strength. Considered a useless and annoying weed by many, delicate Dandelion is a medicinal and nutritious power herb used for healing, food, and tea.

Dandelion translates to *dent-de-lion* in French, which means "the lion's tooth," symbolizing the courage and supremacy of lions. As an emblem of the sun, Dainty Dandelion represents life-giving energy. It is no wonder this modest flower has the power of adaptation!

Children and adults alike enjoy the magickal experience of blowing Dandelion's feathery seed-heads into the wind. Watching the tufts fly, delicate as it may be, Dainty Dandelion's soft flexibility and stamina outlasts many other strong-bodied plants.

"It is not the strongest of the species that survive, nor the most intelligent, but rather the one most adaptable to change," affirms Leon Megginson. Dainty Dandelion takes one into a place of self-creation.

One need not be the biggest and best to live a life fulfilled—just move with the winds of life to succeed beyond personal limitation, and experience well-being.

Dandelion Spirit Power Message

Listen to Me!
I have the Power of Three.
One: be true to yourself.
Two: here you are planted.
Three: spread your light.
Do not expect others to do for you.
This is the losing of self!
You are a Child of the Universe
And life grows within.
In your glory
You shine with the sun.
This is my message to you
Let us be as One!

Dream Song to Adaptation

Dear Dandelion
Your preciousness bespeaks volumes
On how to be.
Strong and sure, flowing free
Even amidst what could feel
The worst place to be!
You show me how to be strong
Yet gentle with beauty.
You show me how it is to feel
Delighted to be.
I do not learn any other way
For you are me.

Thank you, O Dainty Dandelion
For your great Gift of Adaptation

Lucky Ladybug

Gift of Friendship

This lucky little Ladybug has landed here to stay
To make my garden pretty and keep the weeds away.

Anonymous

Sitting atop Dandelion, bright little Ladybug sweetly dances! Ladybug is a beloved and friendly being to many. Even though Ladybug is a North American insect, its minute and creative appearance has made it popular in many cultures over the centuries. With Ladybug's bold winged color, dotted with black spots, one becomes instantly attracted to its delightful appearance. When Lucky Ladybug lands on our body, we smile at its sweet presence, as it makes our heart glad.

Ladybug is harmless to humans, animals, and crops alike. Indeed, it is a boost to a healthy and abundant food chain. Farmers honor Ladybug for its diligent and voracious appetite of damaging insects. Thus, this little beetle has been globally symbolized and respected as good luck.

Ladybug totem shares the element of friendship. This charming being spreads joy wherever it flies. Sharing heart is a message of Ladybug. Playfulness, beauty, and harmony dwell within the spirit of Lucky Ladybug.

Life is enriched by friendship. As we share the beauty of ourselves, we are graced a thousand-fold. Friendship is the sweet nectar of existence. Blessed Lucky Ladybug—an enchanting giant of joyful being!

Ladybug Spirit Power Message

Listen, Friends!
Friendship is a way to let fear fly away!
My presence is of small concern
For the great Divine Heart guides the way.
By my existence I am a friend to life
As I am a sign of nature's love.
Allow yourself to be guided
to the knowing of care.
As there are higher forces out there.
Lucky is the one with friendship.
With others as well as self.
Life is made sweeter by this love-sharing.
You are a radiant being
Of infinite love.
I am lucky to bless you in this way
Our friendship is here to stay!

Dream Song to Friendship

Sweet Ladybug, I see you fly
Your colors bright and bold catch my eye.
I see you doing your miracle work
As a friend to many
O little Ladybug!
Shine my colors, you say,
Let my light shine every day.
Friend to self and others
Is magick, you say.
I aspire to fly on your wings
And bring joy and other sweet things!
You are a grand totem, a gift to remember
You make my heart sing with love—
An eternal ember.

Thank you, O Lucky Ladybug
For your great Gift of Friendship

Ravishing Raspberry

Gift of Manifestation

Manifestation is an act of trust. It is the soul pouring itself out into its world, like a fisherman casting a net to gather in the fish he seeks; with each cast properly made, we will bring what we need to us, but first we must hurl ourselves into the depths without knowing just what lies beneath us.

David Spangler

Among abundant Dandelion, its sister Raspberry grows in delicious spreads. Ravishing Raspberry is a wild being in a crazy riot of manifestation! It grows freely in most areas of forest, grasslands, and almost anywhere roadside.

Berry expressing its sweetness and beauty as an open invitation for feasting—feeding human, bird, animal, and insect. It delights in abundance and lives to manifest. Many of us love to search come spring and summer for this juicy, abundant fruit.

Ravishing Raspberry glows a bright crimson, shining in the Sun in profuse little clusters bouncing in the breeze. This soft little fruit enjoys and lives in sweet expression of bounteous being.

One may look upon Raspberry as the epitome of manifestation, with generous bunches multiplying and thriving during the growing season. Raspberry totem reminds us to bloom who we are, where we are, and become nourishing fruit for life. Enthusiastic Raspberry is wild about self-creation and proof that we may do so.

"You are what you want to become. Why search anymore? You are a wonderful manifestation," states wise Thich Nhat Hahn. Ravishing Raspberry says to *'Grow' for it!*

Raspberry Spirit Power Message

I am alive
I am abundant
I am growth!
Watch me take form
And create and embrace
That which is me!
You are the same life-giving fruit.
As you manifest Self
You bless All That Is.
Grow, blossom, reveal
All that you are and want to be.

Dream Song to Manifestation

Sweet Raspberry!
You, who give us a riot
Of beauty and sweet flavor
Amidst the brambles of life.
You show me presence and abundance
Everywhere.
I learn from you
How to manifest my own self.
And love who I am.
Your delicious sweet charm
Grows in me.
You set me free!

Thank you, O Ravishing Raspberry
For your great Gift of Manifestation

Sentient Seed

Gift of Legacy

> *Your mind is the garden,*
> *your thoughts are the seeds,*
> *the harvest can either be flowers or weeds.*
>
> Wordsworth

As Raspberry flourishes from bud to fruit, it lavishes Mother Earth with an infinite amount of Seeds—microscopic pods of life! Miniscule Sentient Seed is the life-birth legacy of all things.

Every moment contains a Seed of energetic presence. It can either offer an uplifting benefit of growth or a destructive development to oneself, and others. In the eternal balance of life, all leads toward evolution. But, what Seed does one offer is the question, and how will it affect life?

In the world of nature, the sentient animal, plant, and mineral kingdoms become a Seed of their instinctive self. But in the human kingdom, we have the ability of freewill—an aspect of choice. What is the gift we shall give to life? What is our Sentient Seed's legacy?

One may choose to give the gift of loving kindness and compassion. Or, one may choose to give malice and pain. What is expressed in thought can be a precursor of Seed consciousness.

Sentient is a word meaning *conscious, feeling,* and *responsive.* Seed is a nucleus. Sentient Seed is a living perception of who I can be and how I will serve life.

What am I thinking today?

Seed Spirit Power Message

Dear Ones
You are a power of Life!
You are a Creator.
What is your legacy toward evolution?
I range from infinitesimal to great
But size is no matter.
My result is always the same
I produce that which I Am.
What are you?
How is your seed growing?
Flourish in Spirit, dear ones!
The highest version of Self
Is what will serve the legacy of life.
Blessed Be your Sacred Divinity.

Dream Song to Legacy

Dear Sentient Seed
You show me through fruition
What nourishment will be.
My legacy is my best self
Always evolving.
May I be ever conscious
And lovingly plant my seed where I may
In honor of your everlasting energy.
May I be mindful of my
thoughts, words, and deeds.
Are they heartening or transgressing?
Sentient Seed, show me the way to thee.
Every moment help me plant the way to be.

Thank you, O Sentient Seed
For your great Gift of Legacy

Miracle Soil

Gift of Fertility

> *In chaos, there is fertility.*
>
> Anais Nin

Microscopic Seed takes the grandstand in the depths of Soil—and behold, life is born anew! Alchemical transformation takes root in the body of sweet Gaia. This is an act of cosmic creativity, infinitely occurring since the beginning of time on earth.

Miracle Soil is the bed of fertility for dormant Seed. In dormancy, there begins a process of enrichment, as Divine consciousness revives Seed into self-expression. The grand mystery of germination causes sweet fertility to bring forth new growth into being.

What once was latent, now goes thru a magickal transformation of passionate action. This could be viewed as a wild uprising—sparking sleeping Seed into a commotion of growth. Sometimes we all need a little shove!

Life presents countless opportunities for manifestation. These sparks of possibility are offered moment-by-moment. Our Miracle Soil is the bed of life itself. Fertility is the action of choice to nourish the seeds of creation in the Soil of one's heart and mind.

There may be some chaotic moments to balance new prospects—it's a given. Periods of adjustment help us become stewards of our creation. And intuition leads to wisdom. Intuition is the Miracle Soil, and wisdom is fertility. Let them grow!

Soil Spirit
Power Message

I am the field that brings forth creation!
Within you dwells the Miracle Soil of conception.
You are your own life's author.
Bring forth the fertilization of Spirit
To assist in your endeavors.
You are never alone
I am ground for your growth.
Plant your seeds carefully
And cultivate beauty.
They are your living flowers.
Bless your fruition
Child of Life!

Dream Song to Fertility

O Miracle Soil
I plant myself into you.
You show me when to rest
And when to spring forth.
My fertility grows in both fields.
I may feel turmoil in stillness
As well as during growth
But I know your Spirit
Is within my ground.
Your Miracle Soil
Is my nourishment.
As I plant myself into you
I feel your light of virility
Spark my passion and move me upward.
I will grow in Spirit-time with you.

Thank you, O Miracle Soil
For your great Gift of Fertility

Worm Wizard

Gift of Alchemy

*The sight of a worm excites my reverence
more than all the gods men have invented.*

Marty Rubin

Shifting within the soil of earth are great transformers. Worm Wizard is in the depths of alchemy! Every movement of Worm is generating the conception, construction, and birth of nature.

This minute being is a powerful magician! Worm Wizard's work includes increasing the amount of air and water in soil for the creation of a fertile bed of birth—an alchemical process to support the health and growth of plants.

Little Worm assists in the decay of organic vegetation, breaking it down so plants may use it for nutrition. After eating, the castings this invertebrate leaves behind are a valuable fertilizer. Even when Worm Spirit departs earth, its body is excellent fertilizer for our planet.

Worm Wizard is a master alchemist. It is in service to the eternal flow of creation. What an amazing and powerful example is Worm totem—a potent reminder of being in stewardship and nourishment to all life.

Let us make magick! Let us add to the creative abundance and growth of higher consciousness. Let us generate positive transformation. Worm Wizard has spoken!

Worm Spirit Power Message

I am a small spark of life
Yet create infinite light.
I work my magick in the fields of growth.
It is here where you may follow me.
By my gift I feed
That which may be in need.
I initiate alchemy.
Through construction and decay
I design a cosmic elixir of energy in every way.
And so, you, great being
May do the same.
Whatever lifeblood you posses
Design it for growth
In the soil of your consciousness.
Here you may be One with me.

Dream Song to Alchemy

Dear Worm, Master of Life!
Size and form is no matter
During the spark of creation.
You show me how to work Divine Magick.
You show me how to transform.
How I use my heart, hands, and mind
Can be used to fashion light-form.
Your alchemy is the act of love.
Your being is an act of power.
I am humbled by you,
Dear Worm Wizard.
I lovingly convey
How you have truly helped me today.

Thank you, O Worm Wizard
For your great Gift of Alchemy

Amazing Ant

Gift of Ingenuity

The tiny ant dares to enter the lion's ear.

Armenian Proverb

As Worm wends its way through the soil, brother Ant works diligently beside it. Amazing Ant is another burrowing soil engineer, assisting with adding nutrients to aid our ecosystem.

Ant colonies thrive in almost every landmass and ecosystem on earth. Their colonies are described as superorganisms because they succeed at being a unified body, cooperatively together to support the colony. This tiny insect's success in countless environments has been credited to its social system, adaptation, use of resources, and defense tactics. Amazing Ant is truly an ingenuous being!

Not only does Ant thrive through organization, but it communicates together to solve a multitude of problems with interactive teaching. It is no wonder Amazing Ant has been studied by humanity as an inspiration to productive living.

What does Ant totem tell us? That initiative, cooperation, skill, and imagination are precursors to a healthy, thriving, and creative community. Ant's collaborative resourcefulness is the heart of its flourishing personal and global triumph.

Yes, there is a lot to be said about this miniscule insect—courageous, powerful, supportive, inventive. Not a bad role model for humans!

Ant Spirit Power Message

Small but mighty!
My mantra never ceases to be
As it is a part of me.
I show you the way
To reinforce life.
Bind together with strength of purpose.
Whatever skills you possess
Use them to safeguard your nest.
EarthLight is your quest.
All for One, and One for All
This journey should not rest.
You are a creative being
Now put yourself to the test.
We are one in this divine enterprise.

Dream Song to Ingenuity

Sacred Ant, I bow to you.
Your united soul
Is a paradigm of harmony.
Hand-in-hand, I learn to rise
And meet the task of any demand.
It is the opening of eyes and heart
That leads the way
To share a part of, you say
To create a nourishing today.

Thank you, O Amazing Ant
For your great Gift of Ingenuity

Captain Quail

Gift of Focus

*The successful warrior is the average man
with laser-like focus.*

Bruce Lee

As little Ant scampers among the soil, Captain Quail is at full attention on a mission of discipline and dedication. This master of concentration keeps its regiment in line for the work of the day. Nary a one strays under Captain's watchful eye.

I had the great pleasure of watching Quail for many days as they aligned together in search of food. In single-minded effort, Captain Quail would give the marching sound, and the ambling group united in serious order—an army of concentrated beings. Captain Quail resounded its command of focus—no strays would be allowed. And so it was!

Quail totem is a perfect example of using resolute attention to reach one's end desire. Along this path, as Quail maneuvers to stay the course, the journey may alter but the result will be the endgame. In steadfast conviction, one may more easily move in the direction to reach the target. Captain Quail reminds us to keep our eye on the prize with a mindset of diligence. Focus is discipline of spirit.

Bumps along the road may occur, but a tenacity of spirit is at the heart of triumph. As Quail moves in step with determination and fortitude, it does not lead astray. Focus is the forerunner to perseverance, the foundation to realization.

Quail Spirit Power Message

Yes, I am intent.
Yes, I focus on the path.
Yes, I go onward.
And yes, every moment counts.
In your journey to there
Follow me here.
One thought, one mind
One way.
Do not stray.
Follow my lead.
I am a warrior of focus
To meet your need.

Dream Song to Focus

Ho, Quail!
I follow your lead.
I do not question the rocky road
Or spaces in-between.
I remember the intent
And follow your lead.
What makes me continue
Is the straight arrow of inner need.
There is no distress or stumbling
For my eye is on the prize.
I follow your lead.

Thank you, O Captain Quail
For your great Gift of Focus

Gregarious Goat

Gift of Curiosity

But... that doesn't make any sense...!
It does if you're a goat.

Linda Medley

While Quail vigilantly tends to business, Goat bounces hither and thither with glee—so much to see! Gregarious Goat possesses a glorious innate sense of curiosity. Its natural inquisitiveness leads Goat to discover and relish newness in the ever-changing world.

A sociable and expressive being, its natural personality is always open to new adventures. By its endearing nature, Gregarious Goat creates many escapades to experience. As a result, many humans enjoy being around charming Goat who delights in new possibilities of sharing and being.

Playful Goat seems to have the unique sense of not only being curious about life—but *enjoying* it! Goat totem is an excellent example of looking for the newness of creation every day. The world is always in a state of evolution, offering a reprieve from dissatisfaction or boredom.

Monotony is out of the question for Goat! This loveable being moves beyond the uninteresting by its enthusiastic and natural curiosity. May we look through the expansive eyes of Gregarious Goat and see the world always in an eternal state of becoming.

Goat Spirit Power Message

Come one, Come all
There is always a show to behold!
Open thine eyes to curiosity
And it will help you be one with me.
Life does not stop becoming anew.
There is something you can always do.
It will enrich your life
Beyond your dreams of being.
For the world is your oyster
And your pleasure, you see.
Wide open with innocence
Is the way to be.
Life abounds for you and me.

Dream Song to Curiosity

Dearest little Goat
I laugh with glee
When I see you dancing around me!
You tell me what is new
To explore, to feel, to be.
Life is not stagnant
It is the opposite, I see.
I will follow your dance
It will lead me home
With you, I am never alone.

Thank you, O Gregarious Goat
For your great Gift of Curiosity

Beautiful Bovine

Gift of Gentleness

Only the weak are cruel.
Gentleness can only be expected from the strong.

Leo Buscalgia

Goat prances among the fields as Beautiful Bovine contently enjoys the tranquility. Bovine is a creature who serves life by its body sacrifice. There is no greater love. True love is Bovine's gentle generosity.

In past times, Bovine was honored by many as the great being it is. Some indigenous cultures revered it as a holy creature offering the Great Giveaway so others may live. Unfortunately, today this respect is rarely the case, as technical and methodical means have stripped the sacredness away.

In the truest sense, Beautiful Bovine is a divine being through its nourishment of humanity. Bovine is a sacred mother of the world. When its selfless act is honored, one aligns with the natural abundance of the all-inclusive energies of giving and receiving. Giving and receiving is the great balance of living.

The spiritual purpose of Beautiful Bovine's life and death is to teach reverence. Respect this being in prayer and bless the balance by offering the Great Thanksgiving. And so, Bovine may receive this divine blessing in the spirit of love in return. So goes the infinite cycle of giving and receiving.

"I am sorry I had to kill thee, Little Brother, but I had need of thy meat. I will do honor to thy courage, to thy strength, and to thy beauty." ~ Te Ata, Chickasaw

Bovine Spirit Power Message

I am life.
I feed your soul
The opportunity for growth.
I feed your body
The substance of nourishment.
We are here together
To walk the wheel of giving and receiving.
Honor my blood, my body, my soul
Let this become a part of you and know
We are connected.
Do me no wrong.
I am a life sacrifice
And in my generosity
If treated with love
I lay myself down
And we each rise above.

Dream Song to Gentleness

Beautiful Bovine
I bow unto you.
You are a sacred life-giver
One who is true.
I beseech all to know
How you teach us to grow.
For your gentle ways
Are the food for souls.
I honor your great Spirit
O beautiful being
And bow down to you
In gracious giving
Mother of the world.

Thank you, O Beautiful Bovine
For your great Gift of Gentleness

Playful Pig

Gift of Affection

There is no power greater than true affection.

Seneca the Younger

In the fields with quiet Bovine is another beautiful being of great character—Playful Pig. Pig is considered one of the friendliest and most intelligent animals, even more than dogs.

Previously just a farm animal, some humans adopted Pig into their home as house pets. Playful Pig possess a loyal and protective character. With its sweet disposition, it has won the hearts of many as a fun and lovable family member.

Engaging Pig is also one of the more social animals, matching the community structure of primates. It has been known to show some playful trickster tactics to get its share of food. Pig is a sensitive being, even enjoying soothing music and massage.

This endearing animal is a great communicator with a heightened sense of awareness who can be taught many things. Leading a rich emotional life, Pig portrays an enthusiasm for living by its charming curiosity and optimism.

It behooves one to reconsider all preconceived ideas about nature beings. Pig stands as a perfect example of a unique being with a delightful and winning character. Pig totem shows the way to the meaning of love and affection.

Pig Spirit Power Message

Come play with me!
Rub my belly and you will see
I am a lover of life.
My many qualities
Of fun and affection
Is to show you the real me.
Affection is loving the sweetness of presence
In the stream of well-being
Eternally flowing.
I show you with genuine care
That anyone can be loved
For the heart of affection lies within.

Dream Song to Affection

O Sweet Pig!
You show how to play
By your divine innocence, I say.
Your lighthearted countenance
Can be enjoyed day by day.
What you show me
Is a priceless gift
For as you open your affectionate heart
I melt within and feel your beautiful part.
You show me the joy of trust
And learning to put aside fear is a must.
Your charming virtue is a healing balm
And I bow to you as you make me strong.

Thank you, O Playful Pig
For your great Gift of Affection

Sweet Sheep

Gift of Whimsy

Find the whimsy.
If you don't wear a tutu once in a while
life will be the way it's always been.

Deborah Jiang Stein

Following in the good-natured footsteps of friendly Pig, Sweet Sheep frolics gleefully in the fields. Little Lamb is admired for its frisky nature, bouncing around and expressing spirit within.

Not only is Sheep naturally lighthearted, but it also bonds in friendship, and possesses great compassion, sophisticated memory, intelligence, and ingenuity. With these amazing attributes, it is no wonder Sweet Sheep celebrates life!

Whimsy is a quaint act of expressing freedom of the soul. Sweet Sheep knows intuitively that being in a state of celebration is the highest form of gratitude and respect for living—the true heart of the soul.

Sheep totem shows that a little frivolity and fun is a manifestation of *joie de vivre*! Expressing whimsy is a nourishment of the higher self, in pure joy. This is an important message for humanity, who oftentimes dwells in the realms of an overly serious countenance. This can be self-destructive, as within the divine spark of energy there eternally exists a stream of well-being to experience.

Sweet Sheep's gift of whimsy is a lively and amusing antidote to stifling strife and somber temperament that disrupts the flow of vitality to the spirit. Try a little levity more often—it is a miraculous tonic for what ails!

Sheep Spirit Power Message

Yes, I am lighthearted and spirited.
How else does one connect
With the joy of the soul?
It is the job of all to do so!
Do not allow the stress of burdens
Become your status quo.
For lo, you will lose your soul.
Put a bounce in your step once in a while
And see the light shining in your smile.
Do not drag your feet of pain
As this will break your spirit down the lane.
Listen, I say
Find a way!
The quality of your life depends on it.
Do it today.
AHO!

Dream Song to Whimsy

Dear Little Lamb
On your feet you bounce and prance
To the song of living.
By your whimsy, I say
You show me the way
To my soul's delightful growth.
A freedom of self
A soaring of spirit
Is your code of life.
I bow in bliss
To your great joy and wisdom.
It is the way
It is time to play!

Thank you, O Sweet Sheep
For your great Gift of Whimsy

Bountiful Bunny

Gift of Providence

*The moment one definitely commits oneself,
then providence moves too.*

William Hutchison Murray

While Sweet Sheep springs in the fields of time, a little furry creature delights many a surprised soul. Bountiful Bunny makes its appearance as a being of divine providence. With a sensibility of perfect timing, Bunny knows whence and where to gather goodness unto itself.

Bunny has been a fascinating subject of folklore and mythology in many cultures. Sweet Bunny holds the honor of several archetypical characteristics. It is respected as a trickster, being able to outwit predators with its quick and cunning response reactions, which confirms Bunny as a sign of good luck. Well known for its ability to procreate, Bunny also represents a fertility symbol and deity in the creation of the world. Bountiful Bunny is also regarded by some cultures as an emblem of innocence and youthfulness with its loveable presence and ability to move in leaps and bounds.

Providence guides Bunny to its needs and desires. This is the innate awareness of foresight. Providence is Bunny's intuitive sense of what serves its greater good toward self-nourishment. Bunny totem speaks of the power of forethought. This wisdom embraces discretion, anticipation, and preparation.

On the journey of life, it benefits one to take note of Bountiful Bunny's shrewd ways. Bunny does not just sit there looking pretty; rather, this powerful being is making a feast out of the gifts of creation for its well-being.

Bunny Spirit Power Message

Yes, I bounce abundantly
In a pattern that may be undiscerned.
Yet, I move with purpose
This, my mindful path.
Providence is the wisdom of movement.
I possess this simple forethought of growth.
May you follow this passage
In the progress of your soul.
For that which truly serves your welfare
Will benefit all, please know.
For as you advance lively on your way
You share the joy of a good day!

Dream Song to Providence

Sweet Bunny bouncing
You are here to stay!
I watch you go hither and thither
Seemingly heedless and astray.
But now I know the power you possess
Is of the utmost care.
You know exactly where you go
And the abundance you want to dare.
So, on my way to tasting the gifts of life
I will follow your lead
And make it one of generous light!

Thank you, O Bountiful Bunny
For your great Gift of Providence

Rousing Rooster

Gift of Expression

*The meaning of life is contained
in every single expression of life.
It is present in the infinity of forms
and phenomena that exist in all of creation.*

Michael Jackson

As Bunny bounces here and there, Rooster stands cock-sure. We are aware of the dominant and uninhibited presence of this brazen bird. Rousing Rooster is an articulate creature well-known for its early morning ritual of heralding a new day with its loud *cock-a-doodle-doo*. Bold Rooster is not timid about expression!

Such confidence has brought Rousing Rooster to the forefront of many cultures' admiration. Since ancient times, it has been a revered animal. Rooster was rooted into religious belief systems, worship, and ceremony as early as 2,000 BC.

By Rooster's audacious aura, it holds an important place in animism, shamanism, and mythology. Standing bold and courageous, proud Rooster has been depicted in art, as a mascot in the sports arena, on badges, coat-of-arm crests, flags, and other emblems of heritage. From the time of Julius Caesar to the present, Rousing Rooster has represented an honored emblem of valiant and daring behavior.

Rooster totem shows one the art of expression without apprehension. Confidence is a key player in genuine self-expression. It is the knowing of one's true gifts and honoring them for what they really are—part of our divinity. Rousing Rooster leads the way for positive expression of Spirit within.

Rooster Spirit Power Message

I am here to say
Be what you may!
In your pure act of self-expression
Do not hold back
Your conscious contribution.
Bestow the greatness that you are.
Be clear and speak from within.
Herald a new day
With what you need to say.
I stand with you
In your being
On your journey this way.

Dream Song to Expression

O Great Rooster
I hear you loud and clear!
I am among those who have hesitated
But with you near
I feel the loss of fear.
Stand tall with me
As I speak my greater truth.
For as I do so
The light of day can shine on.

Thank you, O Rousing Rooster
For your great Gift of Expression

Garden Gate

Gift of Restoration

*If you long for a mind at rest and a heart
that cannot harden...go find a gate
that opens wide into a secret garden.*

Anonymous

Rooster's call can be heard in the distance through many gardens. As we come to the garden of life, we cross through the Garden Gate. What rich symbology enfolds these words—an illuminating and nourishing sentiment. Restoration is what one seeks and needs in the living of our day.

Walking through the Garden Gate offers an enchanted moment of leaving one world and entering another—from the outer mundane into being untouched by time. It is a moment of divine serendipity, a parting of the veils between the illusions of the material world and the reality of the natural world.

Here, through the Garden Gate, one may experience a restoration of spirit embracing mind, body, and heart. This place between the worlds is a refreshment of comfort, inspiration, and love.

When the strain of life is heavy upon the shoulders, the Garden Gate offers a sweet respite out of the dimensions of time and space. It is a place of inner spiritual and bodily contentment to ease what may weigh heavily upon the soul.

Take thyself into the Garden and restore faith, hope, and love. Lay upon the soft air and listen to the song of Mother Nature rest upon thy soul.

Garden Gate Power Message

I am a door to the beauty of you.
I restore yourself to thee.
Come through my beckoning Gate
Through all time and space
And I will comfort you to feel free.
Loosen the shackles of your day
I am here for you in every way.
Rest down thy bones of weariness
And pain upon thy breast.
Here, through me
You can gain your rest.

Dream Song to Restoration

Through the Garden Gate
I feel myself melt into thee.
You come to open me up
To set me free.
There is a rest beyond the world
And here I sit
With so much peace around me curled.
You have unfettered my foe
Which is me, this I know.
You restore my soul.

Thank you, O Garden Gate
For your great Gift of Restoration

Healing Harvest

Gift of Health

*Let thy food be thy medicine
and thy medicine be thy food.*

Hippocrates

Through the Garden Gate dwells an abundant Healing Harvest. Several years ago I discovered an article called "God's Pharmacy." Its origin, as well as the author, remains curiously unknown. It is a worldwide circulated list that has been integrated into many editorial pieces, including articles in *Time Magazine.*

What is amazing about "God's Pharmacy" is that it packs a powerhouse of information about certain foods whose appearance resemble a part of the body they nourish as a natural tonic. It has been called *"...the sacred geometry of everything. God left us a great clue as to what foods help what part of our body!"* [7] Thus, I dedicate this Healing Harvest journey to the unknown author for his/her astute perception and wisdom.

Excerpt: Walnut—*A walnut looks like a little brain, a left and right hemisphere, upper and lower cerebrums. Even the wrinkles or folds on the nut are just like the neo cortex. Walnuts develop more than three dozen neuron-transmitters (sic) for brain function.*[8]

We have the valuable opportunity to enhance our personal and global health through the consumption of quality earth-grown foods. This Healing Harvest is from the living body of our beloved Mother Earth. We are fortunate to have fresh foods that naturally bestow well-being. A body that is loved and cared for also nurtures one's mental and emotional bodies. Food is a divine alchemist. How blessed we are.

---

7 selfhelphealth.wordpress.com
8 https://faithhealth-wpengine.netdna-ssl.com/wp-content/uploads/files/gods-pharmacy.pdf

Harvest Spirit Power Message

I am the Bread and Breath of Life.
I am a part of your body
To be consumed for your health.
Blessed are we to be One!
Take it upon yourself
To nourish your whole self.
For that which you eat of me
Will become a healing to thee.
Remember, I am born of Mother Earth
Your beloved parent
Who seeks to nourish your growth.
Let us be One
In the healing of all life.

Dream Song to Health

O Blessed Harvest
I am in great gratitude for your presence.
For as you grow, you nourish me
And we become One.
Your life feeds my divinity.
How blessed am I to blossom
With consecrated food, earth's body.
The sacred food of life.
For what comes from Mother Earth
May forever feed the world.

Thank you, O Healing Harvest
For your great Gift of Health

Lovely Lavender

Gift of Attraction

The law of attraction is this: You don't attract what you want. You attract what you are.

Wayne Dyer

One of the many gifts of Healing Harvest is Lavender. Ah, Lovely Lavender. Lavender has been one of the most popular and beloved flowers through history. This aromatic flowering herb has been used abundantly for centuries in countless applications and practices, ranging from culinary use, mental and physical health benefits, aromatherapy, and more.

Possessing a unique scent, Lavender is purifying, herbaceous, and sweetly floral. It grows wild and hardy in many areas and is cultivated in vast fields to be harvested for its many virtues.

Lovely Lavender is a spirited plant of great attraction. Its heady essence is alluring. As one rubs the flower buds between the fingers, a highly aromatic fragrance lingers and delights. This is all a part of Lavender's enchantment.

Lavender totem shares the mystical meaning of attraction. As one is, one attracts. Its message is to aspire to be the greatest version of oneself in the changing landscape of persona. Growing and cultivating one's finest bouquet of self will assist in reaping the experience of drawing to self what nourishes. Lavender Spirit charms life by its mere presence of being, and so may we also.

Lavender Spirit Power Message

I am here to attract.
As I give many blessings
I receive the blessings of many.
You delight in my essence
And I welcome our union
For this is the oneness of being.
In your heart uncover
An attraction of Spirit
For we are all from One
Loving each other as ourselves.
This is good medicine.
Walk within this harmony.
The best that you may be
That is your legacy.
And life will come unto you.

Dream Song to Attraction

O Lovely Lavender
Your beauty beguiles me.
As you give of yourself
You become one with me.
This is an abundant blessing
For my beauty resides in you too.
As I love you, I become a part of you.
This is our attraction
Of one for the other.
In the blending of sweet harmony.

Thank you, O Lovely Lavender
For your great Gift of Attraction

Sunflower Power

Gift of Energy

*The more willing you are to surrender
to the energy within you,
the more power can flow through you.*

Shakti Gawain

Among Lavender's friends is one of the most striking flowers on earth—Sunflower. Sunflower can grow five-to-ten feet tall, with the largest at twenty-six feet. Sunflower's brilliant face of multiple petals, known as rays, distinctly resembles the sun. As our sun is a vital source of life, so Sunflower Power is symbolic of energy. By its act of turning to face the movement of the sun, Sunflower portrays a stunning display of phototropism. We are akin to Sunflower in the receiving of this energetic vitality.

Sunflower is rich in historical and cultural significance. Being a fertile source of nutrients used for food and health, this divine flower is also prevalent and beloved in the world of art and religious symbology.

Following one's inner vitality in the expression of self is an important message of Sunflower totem. This dynamic flower shows that inner strength lies within as a guiding force to create one's life.

It benefits one to explore the divine spark within. Energy leads from the direct source of emotion and passion. "Energy is equal to desire and purpose," notes inspirational writer Sheryl Adams. Aspiring to shine one's light in a beneficial way will guide to true soul expression. Sunflower Power can lead the way.

Sunflower Spirit Power Message

Yes, I am here!
I follow the life of the sun.
In this way, so may you also.
Your sun is within.
It is your power, your energy of creation.
Use it in the highest light
For the nourishment of life.
Here, you will flourish
And grow to your true stature of Self.
I illuminate the way
For you every day.
Do not diminish your presence
For you are a light upon the world.

Dream Song to Energy

O Beautiful Sunflower
You shine so brightly.
You reach for the golden sun
And by your power, follow it through.
May my life be as brilliant as you.
Great Energy Being
I stand before, and with you
As we gaze together
Toward the light of day.
We will be One
As always, this way.

Thank you, O Sunflower Power
For your great Gift of Energy

Honeybee Honor

Gift of Integrity

*One can no more approach people without love
than one can approach bees without care.
Such is the quality of bees.*

Leo Tolstoy

Within the heart of Sunflower, little Honeybee performs a huge job! This buzzing insect diligently flies from flower to flower collecting nectar to produce honey as one of earth's largest pollinator of crops. Not only of major importance in the production of human food, but its honey also holds great medicinal and therapeutic value. Honeybee is the only insect producing beneficial food eaten by man.

Honeybee facts are an astounding tribute to this little insect's honor. It must gather nectar from two million flowers to produce only one pound of honey. When Honeybee discovers a healthy source of nectar, it returns to its hive to share the information by performing a specific dance, which informs the foragers of the position of the flower in relation to the sun and hive.

Clever Honeybee belongs to a social colony consisting of well-organized tasks that support the whole nest. Each insect performs its job in the highly-functioning colony for the good of all. The community of Honeybee has been utilized by theoreticians as a model for human society.

Honeybee Honor certainly holds a high degree of integrity to aspire to. Without Honeybee, life on earth as we know it will rapidly decline—and end.[9] It would benefit us all to deeply respect this tiny being for its authentic devotion and gift to the very core of existence.

---

[9] http://www.bbc.com/future/story/20140502-what-if-bees-went-extinct

Bee Spirit Power Message

We are One
And show the way!
There is no separation between us.
Watch us work and play
For we are One.
Our glory is in the Holy One.
With transcendent power
We build the fabric of One.
You marvel at our diligence
But it is pure joy.
Joy is the light shining within the Heart of One.
For here you will find your glory
Your strength, your virtue.
Follow it all the days of your life
To this Light of One.

Dream Song to Integrity

O Precious Honeybee!
The bringer, the builder, the creator
Of One.
By your Spirit
You show the way
To be in harmony with what comes today.
It is for the good of all
Which must come, if we are not to fall.
Your honor, beyond compare
Will guide me to be thus aware.
For integrity bonds me
To the true harmony of life.
May it ever be so.

Thank you, O Honeybee Honor
For your great Gift of Integrity

Buddha Kitty

Gift of Knowing Now

*What you perceive as precious is not time
but the one point that is out of time: the Now.
That is precious indeed. The more you are focused
on time—past and future—the more you miss the Now,
the most precious thing there is.*

Eckhart Tolle

While Honeybee buzzes around, Kitty sits in deep silence. I watch Kitty in the garden, sitting like the great Buddha, calm and strong of spirit. Buddha Kitty dwells in the now. What is this place of being?

Knowing now is an eternal space of no-time, where the one moment is lived—now. Kitty sees, hears, smells, and feels what is occurring in the present. All senses perceive knowing now.

When Buddha Kitty plays, its whole being is playing now. When Kitty eats, eating becomes now. It does not wonder where the toys are, if it will find a lizard outside later, or feel bothered about the bird that was teasing it yesterday.

What may one remember of the benefits of knowing now? Kitty totem says to let all else go—past and future—unless there is a valuable lesson, or the joy of an experience derived from those two states of being. Memories serve a purpose, but guilt and worry do not. The present moment is where and when all change occurs.

Knowing now is dwelling in a state of freedom, without hindrance of what was, or could be. All else is superfluous. Now is where one is and becomes. Dwell with Buddha Kitty in the priceless moment of now.

Kitty Spirit Power Message

Ah, this holy space is One.
It is now or never!
So, you too should follow this way.
A clear path to the eternal
One moment
Where all life is lived.
In this presence lies your power
As it beholds your soul in the single moment
Always in perfection.
So, do not fret of your tomorrows
And absolutely not of yesterdays
For they are binding chains cursing your heart
And the true freedom of your being.
Let them not covet you as destroyers of dreams
For in the moment, dream of who you are—and be.
Discover this, your golden key.

Dream Song to Knowing Now

O Great Buddha Kitty
I see you dwell now.
There is no other way
To become who I may.
It is only now.
For all the other paths
May lead me astray.
Now is the sacred time
I live and breathe today.
I see you during your day
And you give 100 percent this way.
Fast or slow no matter.
What is valuable
Is not to past or future scatter.

Thank You, O Buddha Kitty
For your great Gift of Knowing Now

Chipmunk Patrol

Gift of Conservation

*Conservation means development
as much as it does protection.*

Theodore Roosevelt

Kitty has captured the hearts of many, and so too has one of Nature's most endearing beings, little Chipmunk. This furry, striped creature goes about its day harvesting seeds and nuts to be stored in its den for intermittent winter hibernation. This activity achieves another important purpose in the ecosystem. Chipmunk's harvesting plays a vital role in seed disbursement, thus enhancing plant growth.

Chipmunk totem is a great preserver. Its service is to itself but also of great benefit to life. Its message is one of caring for self, but not without the mindful presence of serving others. For as the ripple flows outward from the stone thrown in water, so actions radiate and touch others. Conservation is safeguarding what is important for the whole. Each act of true conservation is a creative nourishment of others.

With cheek pouches stuffed with seeds and nuts, archetypal Chipmunk is a tribute to the great act of conservation. Chipmunk ensures its importance by doing its job well. Chirping loudly when threatened at work, Chipmunk Patrol staunchly continues its route of preservation.

As one attends to daily living, Chipmunk skillfully reminds us to be ever-vigilant in the act of safeguarding life. For we are all connected in the earth-web of physical existence.

Chipmunk Spirit Power Message

Yes, I store and protect my fodder.
I am fodder!
As I search and collect for my goods
I myself feed others.
There is no deception in my making.
Care for your needs
But do not displease.
For any greedy action
Will cause a faction.
We serve each other
In the Tree of Life.
Do this without strife.

Dream Song to Conservation

Great Chipmunk Patrol
You know where to go
To plant the seeds of life.
By your astute actions
Of collection and accommodation
You show me a path of sustenance for all.
O Power Animal of conservation
I will readily be aware of care.
Tiny creature with big job
Show me the stewardship way of the great wheel.

Thank you, O Chipmunk Patrol
For your great Gift of Conservation

Bird Psalm

Gift of Hope & Glory

The song of the bird awakens man from his slumber and invites him to join in the psalms of glory to eternal wisdom that has created the song of the bird.

Kahlil Gibran

Among the trees dwelling with Chipmunk, music can be heard from one of life's precious, uplifting beings—behold Bird! What would life be without the beauty of Bird Psalm? Early morn, or through the darkest night, Bird sings its paean to the hope and glory of living.

How and why does Bird sing? Songbird possesses a unique form of anatomy, with a specialized two-sided vocal organ. This allows Bird to create more than one independent vocal pitch at once—a physical symphonic marvel of delicate tones and melodious tunes.

Bird Psalm calls from elevated perches, singing to be heard on high. Often sung in duets, Bird Psalm is also performed in larger symphonic practices to broadcast the message further.

Many ornithologists have conjectured that Bird may sing purely for the pleasure of it. This theory sounds highly plausible, since there is so much beauty in the notes of Bird's arias. It has been accepted that when Bird Psalm is sung without territorial or courtship interests, the splendor of the song and the pleasure of singing could be the reason of expression.

Bird Spirit is a reminder of the pure beauty of song as a guide to the higher worlds of the hope and glory. Always a new day with the early songbird and into the dark night of Bird Psalm, there may always be a reason of discovery for the promise of life's eternal blessings.

Bird Spirit Power Message

Hail Humans!
We are connected by sight and sound
Flying all around.
We sing our song of hope and glory
Where all is possible. We sing as One
And our voice touches all in accord.
We heed you listen!
Our sweetness is borne from the one true heart
For within the notes of our song
It touches a chord as unanimous glory rings true
And the presence of love abounds.
We sing with the sea, and the bee
And the rivers flowing.
With the mountains, and the wolf
And all things in between.
For our song is one with life.
It sings of eternal hope
Springing within the heart of all beings.
Come fly with us and praise heaven on earth.
Glory Be.

Dream Song to Hope and Glory

Sacred Bird, I hear you call
In so many wondrous hymns to all.
You raise me up, you bless me so divine
The highest glory of your Psalm.
I feel exalted in this state
For you have called me into this heavenly place.
Enchanted mantra you do sing
And I bow down to you and bless your wing.
There are no words to describe the love I feel.
For you have sung into my heart and touched my soul.
This is a dream I will always know.

Thank you, O Bird Psalm
For your great Gift of Hope and Glory

Hummer Fuchsia

Gift of Abundance

*Not what we have, but what we enjoy,
constitutes our abundance.*

Epicurus

Among the sweet chords of Bird Psalm, a distinct chirping can be heard—hummingbirds warring against each other over nectar! Abundant Fuchsia, brimming with plump, radiant blossoms, spreads its essence for all to feast. One may muse at the hummers' bold aggression in comparison to Fuchsia, who gives freely of its gracious self.

A brief part of Hummer Fuchsia's life cycle is spent growing delicate flowers from bud to bloom, feeding butterflies, birds, and bees. There is infinite wealth of Fuchsia's life in sweet relationship to nature—it thrives from the gratifying attention of those drinking its nourishment.

Hummer Fuchsia is in ecstasy in the gentle giving of self. Its sweet countenance is charity, and its great gift to the world is the delight of its own bounty. Nectar-rich Fuchsia happily blushes in the sun.

Hummer Fuchsia blesses creation by its illumined inner beauty. It is the epitome of divine love. Through this pure and simple offering of self, one can grasp a more enlightened vision of being. Fuchsia Spirit's message is that we possess the unique treasure of self to share. We can all share a kind word, a loving touch, a heartfelt smile—all these simple acts of charity can be freely given from the grace of our being.

This deep wellspring of inner abundance is infinite. It flows from the greater self in anticipation and joy of the discovery and wealth of our own precious gifts. As genuine offerings from the heart, we bloom through every act of goodwill as we give ourselves in humble grace to all life.

Fuchsia Spirit Power Message

My life is filled with great joy!
As I give, I receive
And all things come back to me.
My flow is within the current of the Universe
Where all energy is abundant.
This vital force externalizes that which is Source
And I have nothing, except to give.
In my richness is my joy, for as I give
I blossom into the beauty of myself.
In this way, you may share love with all that you see.
For it is your crown of glory
And your inheritance, you see.
May this holy life be yours.

Dream Song to Abundance

I flow from the heart of you
O Hummer Fuchsia.
I see your flowers of love
Coming only from above.
It is an outpouring of all that you are.
For as you give, you feed the world
The blessing of your sweet nectar.
I see the purity of heart in all that you do
And will aspire to grow
And blossom like you.
Your radiance of being flows outward
As an abundant eternal light.

Thank you, O Hummer Fuchsia
For your great Gift of Abundance

Rose Divine

Gift of Love

If you are aware that no one else
can make you happy,
and that happiness is the result
of love coming out of you,
this becomes the greatest mastery of love.

Don Miguel Ruiz

Amidst the glory of Fuchsia grows beloved Rose. What flower has been more adored throughout history? The religious symbology of Rose Divine is rich in varied acts of devotion by many world faiths. Its velvety petals and rich fragrance have been created into many artistic, epicurean, therapeutic, and cosmetic products to honor, entice, flavor, heal, and beautify life.

With its beautiful unfoldment of petals and beguiling essence, elegant Rose is hailed as an emblem of love, both earthly and divine. Symbolic of such a high ideal, adored Rose may be viewed as a singularly great gift to humanity.

Meditating upon Rose Divine may bring one into the very heart of unconditional love and pure beauty. Deep within Rose's delicate petals dwells a softness of incomparable depth and exquisiteness—a feeling of being enfolded by divine tenderness. Enfolded by this loveliness in the heart of Rose's heavenly scent one may experience bliss. Here, one may touch the loving essence of Spirit. Love is the passion of compassion, and Rose Divine is a quintessential being expressing this feeling.

As one touches and smells Rose's unrivaled beauty, a deep appreciation may unfold of a glorious presence beyond the physical. One may only smell Rose's perfume and touch its gentle petals in an attempt to absorb its heart of divine love. Blessed Be that Rose elevates me!

Rose Spirit Power Message

My love is your love.
We are one in its presence.
It is a place where all is well
Where you and I truly dwell.
Love is your true home.
You are a fragrance of love
Beautiful and pure.
Healing and heartening
This place Divine.
Think on this, and be pleased
For love is the truth of your being.
Everything else is illusion.
Rest in this and you will be free.

Dream Song to Love

I find, O Rose Divine
That you live in the very heart of me.
You dwell within my blossoming of Self.
For what else am I truly,
Except the budding of love?
You teach me the soft, yet strong way
To flow in the infinite stream every day.
Your divine fragrance beckons me home.
It is the only place to grow and roam.

Thank you, O Rose Divine
For your great Gift of Love

Sacred Prana

Gift of Life

*Best of all is it to preserve everything in a pure
still heart, and let there be for every pulse
a thanksgiving, and for every breath a song.*

Konrad von Gesner

Breathing the heart of fragrant Rose, one knows that Prana is alive. Prana is Sanskrit for *breath*, the Divine spark of energy from whence we all come.

In some philosophies including yoga, meditation, holistic health, and martial arts, Sacred Prana comprises all cosmic energy infused and embraced by universal consciousness. As a subtle quality of the body, Prana has a consciously visible aspect which is the air we breathe. The invisible aspect is the spirited vitality that flows through the body upon breathing. Sacred Prana nourishes in this way.

It is believed that Prana connects the physical, mental, emotional, astral, and spiritual bodies in a unified network as the whole of consciousness. This supports the New Age concept that each living thing, including inanimate objects, is a universe unto itself.

Sacred Prana is vibrant, breathing the gift of life. One may practice the simple act of *conscious breathing* to assist in bringing an awareness of this cosmic spark, the energetic dynamic in all existence. This practice is called Pranayama. It is an exercise that clears obstacles in the physical and subtle bodies and allows the breath to flow Prana—the energy of creation. Through a regular and sustained practice of Sacred Prana, the whole body can be supercharged.

Prana Spirit
Power Message

I Am Life.
I breathe to and through you.
It is from me that you are.
I am the essence of you.
And as we flow together
We ignite eternity!
For your spark is Divine
In the creation of me.
We manifest each other.
Let us dance in this sacred flow
And be One, and know
We are unified together
As it has always been so.
Blessed are you and me.

Dream Song to Life

O Sacred Prana
I feel your power energy within.
It is pulsing and sparking
Life into me!
How can I not know this
Divine aspect of Self?
For within my holy body
We give and receive
Life to one another.
I am you and you are me
Flowing free.

Thank you, O Sacred Prana
For your great Gift of Life

Holy Lotus

Gift of Resurrection

*Dawn and resurrection are synonymous.
The reappearance of light
is the same as survival of the soul.*

Victor Hugo

As Prana breathes into all things, so it is with Holy Lotus. This sacred being of many cultures cultivates, grows, and flourishes within the deepest, darkest bog as one of the most revered flowers. Thus, it is a global symbol of enlightenment.

From the shallow murky waters, the unfolding petals of Lotus open one by one, representing expansion of the soul. From thick sludge, the graceful growth and pure beauty of fragrant Holy Lotus offers the light of hope and spiritual promise.

Lotus holds an esteemed place of honor in classical writings, art, and through verbal exaltations. It is venerated as representing elegance, perfection, purity, and grace. Many deities are depicted holding, enfolded within, or seated on Holy Lotus.

Lotus has the remarkable ability to regulate the temperature of its flowers for maximum blossoming. A single plant can live for over a thousand years and has the rare ability to revive into activity after long periods of dormancy—that is, a seed dated about 1,300 years successfully germinated in 1994![10]

And so, Holy Lotus is seen as resurrection—rebirth from the dark of the night. In symbolic death, life calls us forth to blossom into the ecstatic beauty of self.

---

10   https://yourshot.nationalgeographic.com/photos/7375853/

Lotus Spirit Power Message

Yes, I am here.
In the dark, in the depths
Where there is decline, decay
I am here.
It is from this fertile place of dark
Where I rest before bloom.
Where I shine on thee
For you are me.
You come forth
To unfold.
Absorb your light
And grow to be free.
Resurrection is you and me.

Dream Song to Resurrection

Holy Lotus
I see you shine!
My heart is yours
And yours is mine.
We come from the Source
Of life itself
There is no holding back
From the Divine.
From what seems nothing, and dark
Unfoldment of Self
Is yours and mine.

Thank you, O Holy Lotus
For your great Gift of Resurrection

Luminous Lake

Gift of Reflection

A lake is the landscape's most beautiful and expressive feature. It is earth's eye, looking into which the beholder measures the depth of his own nature.

Henry David Thoreau

Divine Lotus springs forth from the depths of Luminous Lake. This is a place of peace. Life rests within itself in the holy waters of Lake. As one sits, staring at still waters, a panorama of life expression can be seen, heard, and felt. Luminous Lake reflects and expresses beauty—as above, so below.

Lake calls upon one to go within and swim in the waters of reflection. As Lake mirrors the sublime nuances of life above, so one may find the soul during quiet, deep waters.

Movement is natural within and upon Luminous Lake. Creatures skim, splash, or swim in the encircling waters, enveloped in the deep nurturing essence of tranquility. So, one may receive benefit from the stillness of focused introspection within the calm, flowing waters of self.

Lake's reflection is the heavens, transcendent and inspiring. As one sits with Luminous Lake, the contemplative process can offer serenity away from the mundane. Divine harmony dwells here.

Take thyself to thy inner Lake and rest within the gentle waters of the soul. It is a refreshment of self, a soothing balm upon tenacious demands of the mind. Luminous Lake ripples intently, softly, and melodiously into the heart of peace. Reflection balances all things.

Lake Spirit Power Message

I am the power of your soul called forth.
It is here where you may find the link
To your Self.
Do not miss the opportunity
To dwell upon the reflection
Within.
For as you do
Spirit will renew and bless.
It is the only way to form a bond
Between heaven and earth
Within.
Listen now, to the sound of silence
Within.
It speaks volumes in soft whispers
Of your true harmony
Within.

Dream Song to Reflection

O Great Lake
I sit by your soul.
And here it all pours forth.
All the rushes of debris
Pour forth
And smooths upon your soul.
You reflect my inner yearnings
My inner consciousness
My inner being.
I humbly adore you, O Blessed Lake
And lay upon your gentle healing waters.
You are a peaceful place to be
Where life is all harmony.

Thank you, O Luminous Lake
For your great Gift of Reflection

Peacock Pleasure

Gift of Celebration

Be like a peacock and dance with all of your beauty.

Debasish Mridha

At the edge of a lovely Lake, intriguing Peacock drinks from the cool waters. Throughout history, Peacock has fascinated us with its vibrant colors and bold stance of breathtaking beauty.

Humanity has honored Peacock Pleasure dating back to the Egyptian pharaohs, through Greek and Roman myth, and in early Christian paintings and mosaics.

In gorgeous display, Peacock's feathered train is detailed in remarkable iridescent color and elegant geometry. For thousands of years, Peacock has symbolized rebirth and immortality due to its brilliant feathers naturally reproducing annually.

In many cultures, Peacock is a symbol of beauty and a reminder to take pleasure in the finer things of life. Majestically strutting a flowing train of dazzling feathers with regal expression, this luminous being proudly shares its animated vitality. Peacock Pleasure represents the celebration of living.

Peacock totem reminds us of the unique splendor of creation. And by sharing its magnificence, this divine being blesses and enhances the glory of living. Bold Peacock bursts forth and expresses life's wondrous glory, revealing life's admiration of itself.

Peacock Spirit Power Message

You come upon my spirit of beauty
And are entranced by me.
I flow within your heart
With the promise of your own enchantment.
You are a Blessed Being
Of loveliness, power, and majesty
Celebrate yourself!
You are a gift to the world to be shared
And you will not find yourself until you do.
Let it come forth from every spark within
And let it shine upward and outward
For your true beauty is unique
Within the realm of life.
It always has been
And will always be so.
Let it shine and flow.

Dream Song to Celebration

O Majestic Peacock
You radiate all the colors of the world!
In brilliant display
You show me how to shine.
Whatever my light is
You show me how to shine.
I am a wonderful part of the world.
I add to the glory of life.
With my luminous feathers of beauty
I share light into the world
And celebrate the Divine within.

Thank you, O Peacock Pleasure
For your great Gift of Celebration

Endearing Elephant

Gift of Compassion

*If anyone wants to know what elephants are like,
they are like people, only more so.*

Peter Corneille

In the land of Peacock dwells another luminous soul. If there is one animal who stands out as possessing deep compassion, it is Endearing Elephant. This great being shares a complex range of emotions parallel to humans—especially care, sympathy, and respect. Elephant possesses profound heart-memory and emotion and does not hesitate to share its deep love and communion through the interdependence of creation.

Countless stories have been shared about Elephant's empathy, and humans have been brought to a greater understanding of the consciousness of the animal kingdom through Elephant's engaging heart.

One such story is about Lawrence Anthony, a South African legend and author of *The Elephant Whisperer*, who devoted part of his life to Elephant rescue and rehabilitation at his Thula game reserve.

Two days after Mr. Anthony died in 2012, Elephants on the reserve came to his home to pay their respect. Led by two matriarchs and walking slowly for days in solemn procession over twelve miles, thirty-one elephants from two herds came to honor Mr. Anthony. They stayed for two days and nights without eating. They had not been to Anthony's home in over three years. How did they know?

Some say the heart of this enlightened being is of great spiritual intelligence and insight. "If there ever were a time, when we can truly sense the wondrous 'interconnectedness of all beings,' it is when we reflect on the elephants of Thula. A man's heart stops, and hundreds of elephants' hearts are grieving. This man's loving heart offered healing to these elephants, and now they came to pay loving homage to their friend," intuits Rabbi Leila Gal Berner.

Elephant Spirit Power Message

I am yours
I give my heart to you.
I show you the way.
No matter what ails
I show the way.
Compassion is your soul's name.
You and love are one and the same.
It is the only worthy game.
Listen to me roar!
I am trumpeting the call
Come and follow my lead.
Drink from the pool of compassion
And feel your thirst no longer.
For you and I are one and the same.

Dream Song to Compassion

O Sacred Elephant
I bow before your great heart!
You show the true heart's holy grail.
Great compassion is yours.
I have much to remember
By your blessed act of Self.
Devotion, kindness, sympathy
Are divine virtues of life.
Forever grateful, forever humble
I stand before your gift
And infuse it into my heart.

Thank you, O Endearing Elephant
For your great Gift of Compassion

Sage Sloth

Gift of Purpose

> *Nature does not hurry,*
> *yet everything is accomplished.*
>
> Lao Tzu

While Elephant walks the solid ground, Sloth hangs from above. Sloth is an arboreal mammal who appears to lead an uneventful existence. Slow moving, hanging from trees, eating, sunning, and sleeping are the basic activities of its life. Sloth is perceived as being sluggish and clumsy. Some believe it is one of the simplest mammals on earth. One could say Sloth moves so slow it gathers moss.

But Sage Sloth is one of nature's miracles. It has a special symbiotic relationship with green algae, which grows on its fur. Sloth has developed an unusual system of camouflage from predators in the trees by naturally infusing its fur with the microorganism. Sloth's algae garden also benefits many insects who obtain shelter in its fur—even birds harmlessly nibble on the nutritious ecosystem growing on this sweet mammal's lush coat.

We are wisely and quietly being shown by Sage Sloth that what may appear to be without benefit can, in truth, be a powerful value to life. Divine purpose always provides a service of growth to many.

As one ponders this sometimes subtle, yet compelling fact, doors of perception can open to embrace all creatures, great and small. There is no insignificant being. Mother Nature is inclusive in her blessing to all creation.

Sage Sloth
Power Message

O humanity, heed me, listen!
I am a simple soul of power.
By my very existence, many thrive.
It is the symbiotic way of creation
that nourishes all.
Balance your thoughts and activities
To include a synergistic frame of mind.
Nurture mutual care for all beings
For all are interdependent.
Embrace the oneness of natural cooperation
For life blesses this simple way.
It is a Divine Purpose, you see
For you and me.

Dream Song to Purpose

O Sage Sloth, you show the way
To sustain and nourish together.
How can it be another way?
It is meant to be effortless, from the heart.
A natural coexistence of purpose.
For we walk, swim, fly, inhale, exhale
and dwell together.
The simple truth of our existence
Connects all to each other.
Even in death, Mother Nature nourishes
So be it, Blessed Be.

Thank you, O Sage Sloth
For your great Gift of Purpose

Ancient Iguana

Gift of Perception

That is exactly how people beat Chinese handcuffs. They turn into Iguanas.

Rick Riordan

While Sloth has captured the heart of many, Iguana has mystified. Ancient Iguana is an otherworldly creature with seemingly magickal powers. Fossil hunters recently discovered it roamed earth before the dinosaurs became extinct ten million years ago... quite an ageless being of shrewd survival instincts.

Iguana has exceptional eyesight, capable of seeing ultraviolet wavelengths. Besides a powerful scope of vision, this primordial lizard possesses an uncanny feature of distinction: a third eye, or *parietal* eye, on top of its head. Although not a traditional eye, its main function assists in the detection of movement and light/dark patterns. As an insight to preservation, the photo-sensory eye registers change to alert Iguana for its optimal welfare.

Iguana totem reminds one of the benefits of perception birthed from sensitivity. As a perfect creation, the third eye enables great Iguana to survive since prehistoric times in the harshest jungles.

Many world philosophies note the third eye, or mind's eye, as a distinctive sense of awareness to "see" through physical reality. The inner eye opens doors to higher consciousness for personal, spiritual and psychological benefit. Iguana Spirit exhibits the art of thriving by perceiving nuances with clarity and then acting as a result of awareness. Sit a spell, take note, and see what is within and around you—a strategy for peaceful living.

Iguana Spirit Power Message

AHO, I see thee!
Through my mind's eye
Through the mist of subtlety
and distinction I see.
To be present at once is the key.
Nuances come and go before thy face
Allow time to observe the landscape.
When deciding a course
Cultivate clarity before action.
Register refined movements of energy
Mindful presence will assist thee.
When observation is clear
Move with insightful reaction.

Dream Song to Strategy

O Ancient One
To be keenly aware
Embraces an inner and outer world.
A blending of vision.
I see your stance, Iguana
And learn from you what to do.
In your stillness of movement
To deliberate action
You exercise shrewd perception
Of far vision.
Lead me there, great Iguana
So I may see and be with thee.

Thank you, O Ancient Iguana
For your great Gift of Perception

Shaman Snake

Gift of Liberation

*Just as a snake sheds its skin
we must shed our past over and over again.*

Gautama Buddha

In the land of Iguana, another reptile draws mystical attention—Snake. While man and animal shed our skins in an inconspicuous ongoing process, Snake profusely sheds two-to-four times per year. Shaman Snake is even more unique because its skin usually sloughs off in one piece.

This distinctive reptile sheds to allow for ongoing growth, as well as to remove parasites attached to the old skin. Unlike humans, when Snake grows, its skin stretches to the point where further development is not possible. At this time, a new layer grows underneath, preparing for release of the old until it is complete. Then the shedding process begins anew.

Shaman Snake has been symbolically honored throughout history by many cultures as a healing totem. One reason is its perpetual innate process of releasing what does not serve its evolution.

One of the major practices in many shamanic cultures is the conscious release of thoughts, words, and deeds that hinder growth. As Nietzsche stated, "The snake that cannot shed its skin perishes." This insight relates to holding onto old patterns of being that have outlived their benefit.

Personal evolution is a key to well-being. Breaching the old ways of being with the ability to recognize and discard the source is a life practice enabling one to reach their potential more easily in the continuous journey of self-discovery and growth.

Life is eternal change. When one realizes that releasing old or detrimental habits promotes growth, half the battle is won. Then the journey begins to make way for new beginnings.

Snake Spirit Power Message

I slither out of my skin
To begin again, to become anew.
This practice I readily do.
It enhances my growth to be.
Without it, I would perish, you see.
Step into your new skin
Let it be thee.
For as you grow and become
A new vision and purpose will serve thee.
It is a step of bravery
To be born anew.
By leaving the old behind to grow
You will walk with me, it is true, I know.

Dream Song to Liberation

O Shaman Snake
I know your ways.
I have walked with you many days.
Even through the fear of change
I see healing come in many ways.
Release, release, release
What serves no more.
For how else can I grow through stagnancy
To evolve anew.
There is no way but to shed the old.
Put on the armor of courage
And go with that flow.

Thank you, O Shaman Snake
For your great Gift of Release

Shifting Dunes

Gift of Change

> *Yesterday I was clever,*
> *so I wanted to change the world.*
> *Today I am wise, so I am changing myself.*
>
> Rumi

Snake moves through the Dunes, while the Dunes of the earth shift through the sands of time. It is said that the only thing that doesn't change in life is change itself. This philosophy may be perceived as esoteric, but in true perception, even atoms embrace the dance of change.

How challenging it feels sometimes to flow or even shift. Look at the beauty of the Dunes... ever-changing to form new horizons, new paths, new journeys. The beauty of Shifting Dunes is created through the gift of change.

In physical geography, Dune is a hill of loose sand built by aeolian processes or the flow of water. Visually stunning patterns are eternally created through the constant flow of sand intertwined with air and water.

Dunes dwell worldwide. Shifting Dunes offer a stunning imagery for life's changing patterns. As we transform through time, we may follow Dunes and grow richer in an endless pattern of our evolution. We have the choice to blossom through Dune's consciousness.

Transformations come and go—sometimes subtle and at other times a harsh revolution of self. Awareness of the flowering potential of personal unfoldment through change can help ease the fluctuating energies.

Look to Shifting Dunes as a vast, elegant reminder of the importance of change. Stagnation does not speak nature's name—what appears to be placid is teeming with dynamic energy.

Dunes Spirit Power Message

I am as vast as the sky
Like the clouds I drift and ever-change.
I am here to tell you of your constant beauty.
Harsh winds may scatter you to pieces
But you may soon gather anew
Even more powerful, more glorious, more alive.
The old patterns must go
It behooves you to flow.
Shifting sands create energy vortexes
For new ideas of life to grow.

Dream Song to Change

Here I am, again, in the throes of change!
How do I stabilize, gain a foot
And stay in the game?
What you say, O Shifting Dunes
Is to follow the patterns of change
And see what growth can be gained.
I bow to you, O Dunes, for your ancient wisdom
For you, by your constant movement
Ground me in the game.

Thank you, O Shifting Dunes
For your great Gift of Change

Calming Palm

Gift of Relaxation

> *Take rest; a field that has rested*
> *gives a bountiful crop.*
>
> Ovid, Roman Poet

As Dune shifts in the wind, Palm dances with the flow. Calming Palm is symbolic and reminiscent of grace—the natural movement of life. Quintessential Palm is the image of a tropical paradise of leisure. Palm's leaves sway and dance in the breeze, beckoning one to *just be.*

And how does one achieve this flow? The gift of relaxation is essential. Amidst what can sometimes feel hectic, Palm reminds us of the vital importance of balancing the flow of activity with repose. Through this alchemical blend, we are able to replenish mind, body, and soul, and nourish self.

In Judaism, Palm represent peace and plenty. As we gift ourselves with rest, peace of mind has a better capacity to enrich into our lives. When heartsease is experienced, a feeling of abundance may naturally enfold us... a feeling of being at one with the world.

Calming Palm has a history as old as the first societies. The Romans gave Palm branches as a symbol of triumph. When we are able to step outside a demanding life and bless ourselves with the gift of relaxation, this truly is a triumph. For we are allowing ourselves to attract and radiate tranquility into the world. Quietude is a place of power.

Take a breather more often. Anoint yourself with this replenishing gift and open the doors to serenity. Become like Calming Palm and *let it flow!*

Palm Spirit Power Message

I am strong and wise
Watch me flow!
This is a place where you can go
To grow.
As you balance all parts of your being
You align with the spirit of all things.
Intersperse your time with moments of calm
For this is a secret and a beneficial balm.
Like the fronds of my treetop
Gently swaying in the breeze
Become one with me.
Take heed of this vibrant mode.
To live your life in this way
Is truth be told.

Dream Song to Relaxation

In this realm of rest
Sometimes it feels a test.
Let it go, and let it flow
Can be challenging, I know.
But I look to you, O Peaceful Palm
For your words do lead the way.
The poise of living may be tricky
But I hear what your words say
As your Divine being points the way
To a wholesome life lived in equanimity.
I exalt myself with rest.

Thank you, O Calming Palm
For your great Gift of Relaxation

Sea Mandala

Gift of Unity

We are each other's harvest;
we are each other's business;
we are each other's magnitude and bond.

Gwendolyn Brooks

Palm flows with the breeze from Ocean's breath. Ocean is a magnificent being. My first significant encounter with nature's consciousness began on a cool summer afternoon along the Oregon Pacific Coast.

As I strolled along the glistening sandy shore breathing the refreshing air, hypnotic waves gracefully flowed. I felt one with the gentle current and reflected on the timeless rhythm of ebb and flow.

Each wave, distinct unto itself, embraces the shore in the pure pleasure of its own being. Yet the vast sea calls it home, over and over, into the depth of one Ocean.

I pondered this miraculous act of unity occurring ad infinitum. Leaving the sea, the rushing wave expresses itself and then elegantly surrenders back into the magnificent fullness of Sea Mandala—to the expansion of self. Like the ancient mandala with its power center symbolic of creation and integration, the Sea is a source of life, energy, and renewal for each wave.

A sense of calm pervaded me in this pure expression of the universal truth of oneness. Unity is the core of consciousness. Its presence is crystal clear and undeniable. Unity is the cohesive cosmic web holding life together.

Like the fluid waves, expression flows outward from one. Dwelling within this truth is a pure expression and devotion to the wisdom of harmony. Evolving as a whole, the fountain of Spirit naturally rejuvenates the whole. This is the weaving of conscious interconnection. This is soul stewardship. This is the self-nourishment. Sea Mandala invites us to flow within the realms of one.

Sea Spirit
Power Message

Come into my essence
Where you can hear the song of eternity
The Unity of One.
The flow of being
Where all are connected.
The smooth sands at your feet
Are a path to me.
Release the ecstasy within and lay thyself down
Upon the soft sands of time.
You can hear my voice within the shores of your Self.
Hear the song of your soul within the eternal flow.
You are at one with me.
All life comes together
Whether you know it or not.
As you embrace this, you shall be forever free.
It is now peace that I share with thee.

Dream Song to Unity

The Song of the Sea
Is calling to me.
In the waters of time
All may be free.
What this entails
Is for me to be one with you
And you with me.
It is a kinship of heart
Which calls to me.
It is the Divine Spark of Life
Through one eternity
Uniting hearts together, Blessed Be.

Thank you, O Sea Mandala
For your great Gift of Unity

Trickster Octopus

Gift of Wit

Wit makes its own welcome and levels all distinctions. No dignity, no learning, no force of character can make any stand against good wit.

Ralph Waldo Emerson

In the great Ocean depths, infinite beings dwell. Long before life on land progressed, Octopus arrived on earth some 296 million years ago. This cephalopod is viewed with wide-eyed wonder as an alien-looking creature possessing a wondrous capacity of intelligence and extraordinary personality. Octopus's impressive navigational abilities, predatory techniques, and communication skills are widely acknowledged.

Trickster Octopus can burst out of its aquarium tank, slip its body through a plumbing hole, and find its way back to the ocean. It can take apart the plumbing and block the outflow, causing flooding. Mischievous Octopus can escape its tank to eat fish in an adjacent tank and return before anyone notices. When the crafty cephalopod recognizes specific people, it squirts them with water. This cunning creature can jet water to turn off spotlights while watching people scramble to fix them, again and again. Then Trickster Octopus steals the overhead cameras to cover up its crime!

In mythology, folklore, religion, and psychology, a trickster is a classic character of great intellect and secret knowledge. It is an archetypal rogue of the collective unconscious who shatters old paradigms and playfully pokes at rigid beliefs and pretensions. Through its crazy wisdom, trickster playfully disrupts normality to abolish decrepit ideologies in order to be re-established in a new way. This shrewd being challenges us to bring fresh awareness in order to change stagnant patterns of thought. Trickster Octopus ultimately raises consciousness. Its antics are a catalyst that point to the path of examination for the necessity of adjustment.

NATURE SPEAKS

Octopus Spirit Power Message

I am to be reckoned
I am to be seen!
With my many arms
By my wit
I point to the light of insight.
Be astute!
I break down the mold of status quo
To create anew
For the flourishing of life.
I chaos the comfortable
To expose the underbelly of perception.
Trickster Seer, yes, I be
To shake up the old way
And align you with me.

Dream Song to Wit

How may I match thee, O Octopus?
Your wit is astounding!
If mine as sharp be
I would surely move with thee.
I endeavor to be clever
To perceive cause and effect.
For by my wit I may make changes
To worn beliefs and perceptions.
Sometimes a breakdown is a breakthrough.

Thank you, O Trickster Octopus
For your great Gift of Wit

Soaring Seagull

Gift of Ascension

*All levels of ascension involve
letting go of things that hold you back.*

Lenon Honor

While Octopus swims deep in the sea, Seagull majestically ascends above. Soaring Seagull is either honored or defiled by humans. Some view Seagull as a pesky scavenger or a magnificent creature defying all physical elements.

Here is the beauty of both: While the seabird may carouse within large, noisy flocks and congregate in public places where food is available, Soaring Seagull is nobly performing a valuable community service. It is the great garbage collector! Foraging on dead animals and organic litter, Seagull prevents what could pose a health threat to humans. Soaring Seagull debunks the erroneous idea of nuisance and ascends as a respected public servant. AHO!

Seagull is an acrobat in the sky. It makes seemingly impossible stunts appear effortless, gliding and soaring for long periods of time, performing buoyant aerodynamic feats. In precision mastership, Soaring Seagull catches thermal wind currents, drifting motionless high in the sky—a master of ascension.

Another amazing feat of Seagull is its staunch hardiness to withstand the most dismal day along coastal shores. Amidst fierce storms, severe winds, and extreme temperatures, Seagull can be seen huddling together with its mates along the seashore, surviving the harsh elements.

Soaring Seagull's gift of ascension is a humble tribute bestowed upon life. Against all odds, this benevolent being shows the way to not only endure, but to triumph. We may look to Seagull as a powerful example of overcoming obstacles to rise anew.

Seagull Spirit Power Message

I take the day as it comes
In any way.
For I am a beneficiary of life.
The cold, the old, the hard, the scraps
The sun, the wind, the joy, the play
I take it all.
And flourish!
Follow me with dignity
For that is your wing
To alight your day.
You will conquer and befriend
And thrive along the way.
Heed me and do this today.

Dream Song to Ascension

O Great Seagull
Flying high in the sky.
Showing your true colors
Of grit and sway.
I look to you for the way.
Stand firm, look high
See the light in the sky.
For you hold the key
To be the best of me.

Thank you, O Soaring Seagull
For your great Gift of Ascension

Darling Dog

Gift of Joy

> *Rhapsodizing! It seems to me both touching and strange that she should find the world so wonderful!*
>
> J.R. Ackerley, *My Dog Tulip*

Have you ever witnessed Dog running free, chasing Seagull? *Joie de vivre* is the theme song of Darling Dog. I have watched Dog's vivacious, unbridled happiness with wonder. How this beautiful being expresses bliss is a full-body experience. Dog cannot contain itself when the happiness of love is within—every muscle jumps for joy!

Darling Dog is an exquisite example of living in the moment and partaking in the beauty all around. Dog knows how to breathe life fully. Every cell is bursting forth with the spark of divine joy.

I suggest that everyone go to a place where Dog may run free—park, beach, etc.—and watch intently the love emanating from this spirited being. As one truly sees, one truly feels, and the effect is contagious. You may just break out in full-body laughs!

This kind of true joy is love... being in love with who you are, what you are doing, and where you are. It is a purity of presence, a vibrant expression of oneness with All That Is, the ultimate celebration of living and the freedom of the soul. Darling Dog is the personification of joy.

As Dog is infused and enthused with joy, it sparks the energy of creation. Dog's ignited passion can catapult one into an energetic state of elation, raising one's vibration to a higher state of being.

When Darling Dog is full-bloom in joy, its body smiles and giggles and cannot contain its effervescence within. Delight in the positive energy of Adorable Dog and you will infinitely be rewarded.

Dog Spirit Power Message

Joie de vivre ~ happiness is love!
I run to you with these words of power and truth.
Let them be your constant guide
In all your dreams and perceptions.
For they rule the day and crown you with purpose.
I come to you full of the power of your soul.
I Am Joy is your soul's name.
Run free with me, let everything be
Joy will carry you home.
For as you feel, so shall it be.
Joy, the Dance of Life.

Dream Song to Joy

O Darling Dog
How I embrace your heart!
You are the wonder-maker, the soul of dreams.
For we all seek the joy you bring.
As I dance and follow your footsteps
I am lighter than air.
My very breath feels joy!
Your passion awakens all the good in life.

Thank you, O Darling Dog
For your great Gift of Joy

Peaceful Pampas

Gift of Grace

> *Grace is the beauty of form
> under the influence of freedom.*
>
> Friedrich Schiller

While Dog runs free along the shore, Pampas flows free in the breeze. Elegant Pampas Grass gently sways in the cool, crisp air along sandy dunes. One may be mesmerized in the reflection of its ethereal beauty—at one with the elements and gently, gracefully dancing.

Life moments come and go, and it's beneficial when one remembers to flow. Times of pain and times of joy all blend into the movement of living...the choice to experience everything as a gift, a learning thing. With a step taken back, another side of life may be seen in clarity. Time spent in graceful repose can guide one towards a better way to go. Not everything is a forward rush. Nature grows and dwells in grace—even storms have their dance.

Confusing moments of uncertainly can become the building blocks to a positive power forward. One may learn to view them as a secret key toward blessed moments of private peace. The world is talking, and I want to listen. Reflecting upon one's path, gently moving forward, eases one into a flowing stance and a true appreciation for all life's moments.

Pampas Spirit expresses the inherent dignity in flowing. It takes a strong, calm soul to flow through life's changes. The resolute outcome is peace within. May it be so.

Pampas Spirit Power Message

You, who are the soul of nature
Come visit my dance.
You see me dancing with the air
And the earth below
And wonder at my beauty.
I am that part of you who surrenders to life.
I surrender to living.
You, who get caught in discontent
Forget your holy being within.
You, whose soul dwells within
My waving feathered leaves
Need not resist this flow any longer.
You may be free, you may let go
You may release all that cringes your heart.
For your spirit is free!
It is flowing in the One Sea of Life
Forever flowing—this is your grace.
Be at peace, my child.

Dream Song to Grace

Sweet Sacred Pampas
You flow to and through me.
I watch you undulate with exquisite grace.
Your feathers touch my soul.
I experience your Divine essence
Of softness and willingness
To flow through life's path.
Wherever it may lead, there I be
To anoint the holy core of myself
In the unfoldment of me.

Thank you, O Peaceful Pampas
For your great Gift of Grace

Queen Anne's Lace

Gift of Elegance

For me, elegance is not to pass unnoticed but to get to the very soul of what one is.

Christian Lacroix

While Pampas bends in the breeze, its sister, Queen Anne's Lace, stands stately tall. Beauteous Queen Anne's Lace can be found growing prolifically in wild fields, inland meadows, and coastal areas. It is not easily missed as it may grow over three feet tall. Standing upright with much poise, Queen Anne's Lace is indeed a stately plant. With the appearance of exquisite white lace, oftentimes it has a solid purple flower within its center—the color of royalty.

Queen Anne's Lace earned its name from a legend that tells of Queen Anne of England pricking her finger while sewing white lace which was stained by a drop of blood. Thus, the tale established Queen Anne's Lace as a flower of nobility.

There is no denying the refinement of this striking plant. Its white crown of tiny clustered flowers stands prominent on stiff thick stems. It is not one to readily bend in the wind. We may indeed perceive Queen Anne's Lace as an excellent example of maintaining personal stature and power.

We are all imbued with the distinction of majesty. It may be veiled, but it is the spirit of each soul. Queen Anne's Lace tells us to stand tall with dignity and be conscious of our inner splendor. It is our right, our divinity. The gift of elegance grows from within, and its seed is the majesty of love.

Queen Anne's Lace
Spirit Power Message

Lo and behold, you are the elegance of the universe!
Take your inner power and walk forth
For you are called to stand tall
And be the might of your soul.
This is the message I bring to you.
You are made of the Divine Spark
This has been foretold.
Wear your badge of glory and follow your path
For you may light the way of many.
Blessed Be, Your Majesty.

Dream Song to Elegance

Divine Queen Anne's Lace, I hear your call.
It is the proclamation of holiness.
It is the gentility of dignity.
Your voice speaks of the purity of Self
Of who I am, and what I am to be.
For as I see your elevated stance
In the wild fields of life
I may aspire to be my own hero
And walk the fearless path of my noble heart.

Thank you, O Queen Anne's Lace
For your great Gift of Elegance

Dolphin Dance

Gift of Magick

Dolphins speak to us of the rhythm of our emotions: breathing in joy before plunging into the depths and rushing to the surface to do it all over again.

Unanimous

Queen Anne's Lace sways with the dance of Dolphin. Dolphin has long been expressed throughout history, religion, and mythology as a shamanic totem in relationship with humans. There exists an age-old fascination with Dolphin, not only as a species of high intelligence but also of possessing a healing power.

The popularity of inter-species interaction with Dolphin greatly increased in the 1980s due to personal connections that many humans experienced. Swimming with Dolphin is of unique interest, and numerous people claim to have been healed of depression or other ailments in Dolphin's presence.

We perceive Dolphin Dance as a pure act of joy and harmony with the environment. It may be perceived as a contagious state of being! Dolphin appears to be eternally smiling, and this physical appearance may indeed infuse magick into one's life.

While there is no hard, scientific evidence that Dolphin may heal, many people who spent time in its presence claim this experience because they felt the energetic exhilaration of Dolphin Dance. They opened themselves to its healing magick.

We have yet to understand the deep therapeutic value of living in kinship with the animal kingdom—not only for personal healing benefits, but for harmony within the great web of creation.

Dolphin Spirit Power Message

Yes, I swim in the great waters of life.
I am here to please.
My magick exists through my perception of being
As I dwell within the infinite flow.
This perception of eternity can enlighten you to grow.
Know, as the ocean waves roll
That you are a precious drop of life's soul.
Here me as I chirp and sing
This truth you should know.
Let it wash over you, over and over
Until you become One with the flow.

MESSAGES FROM THE CONSCIOUSNESS OF OUR WORLD

Dream Song to Magick

Great Dolphin, I see you smile!
Forever you are letting me know
Life is a great rhythm of ebb and flow.
You play with the lightness of being
That is your magickal healing.
For as you swim to the dark depths
So, too, you come bouncing to the surface
Expending extraneous energy into the waters of time.
Letting all go to be present in your joyful moment.

Thank you, O Dolphin Dance
For your great Gift of Magick

Whale Wisdom

Gift of Knowledge

*Wisdom and deep intelligence require
an honest appreciation of mystery.*

Thomas Moore

Dolphin dances in the same waters as Whale journeys. Magnificent Whale has been feared and revered by man since ancient times. Portrayed as monstrous, as well as benevolent, Whale has been perilously close to extinction throughout history, yet shines as a Gentle Giant.

Whale Wisdom is as ageless as time. We may look to this benevolent soul as one who holds a key to living. To going back to nature. To retrieving indigenous ways of being, and honoring life. To singing the song of life.

The way of true knowledge is the way of intelligence. The way of intelligence is the way of wisdom. It is an endless circle of soul expression. As Whale Wisdom flows through the waters of time, its vast presence swims in kindred space with the timeless. And the mystery of the creative universe abounds.

We may speak to Whale Spirit. In this sacred space, we flow within the all-encompassing embrace of divinity. Whale Wisdom can take us there. As we journey with Whale through the ocean of time, through the mystery of higher consciousness, we may retrieve our eternal soul.

This is the beckoning of cosmic knowledge. The mystery unfolds, reveals, and embraces us. Riding with Whale Wisdom, we swim through the waters of creation and know the vastness of one.

As social scientist Nicholas Lore proclaims, "Everyone else on the planet, from the lowest amoebae to the great blue whale, expresses all their component elements in a perfect dance with the world around them."

This is a key to living. May Whale energy abound in your dance as you swim though all waters, high and low.

Whale Spirit Power Message

Listen, listen!
I sing the Song of Life so that you may grow.
I am here to guide you to the edge of your dreams
So, you can let them go.
Free they will be.
You dwell within the mystery of knowledge.
This is where the beginning and endless flow.
It is an opening of your heart
To go into deep waters.
As you gain wisdom there, then may you rise
In self-expression with the joy
Of creation in your song.
It is the hidden depths where I go.
Remember this, and you will know how to grow.

Dream Song to Wisdom

Mighty, magnificent Whale!
Swim into my life and take me low
Into the deepest waters of my soul.
For I can hide no longer, I need to open wide.
It is becoming a part of the whole world.
It is being in the depths
With this knowledge of living.
And I know it is here, where I tread and retrieve
The lost fragments of me, my soul.
Then may I rise in exuberance
And express the true joy of being.
For your wisdom is this knowledge
And I swim with the world around me.

Thank you, O Whale Wisdom
For your great Gift of Knowledge

Geese Fortitude

Gift of Perseverance

*Attitude with gratitude supported by fortitude
will take you to the next altitude.*

Bayode Ojo

While Whale swims deep, Geese fly high above. Geese is a marvel in flight. We look above, in awe of their focused determination. Honking on course, Geese fortitude sets sight on a mystery flight of life.

> *The longest stream of Geese I've seen
> In graceful flow trailing the sky
> Undulating in countless numbers
> A living ribbon on the wing on high.
> Voyaging over ocean waves
> A visual symphony in flight
> Their shape of being creating
> Fluid curves sailing the sky.
> This nautical journey to terra firma
> Across a myriad of bountiful miles
> With mysterious sense of purpose
> The endurance of spirit survives.*

What is the enigma of Geese's flight? It travels by orienting itself to magnetic fields, the sun, air currents, and speeds and changes in the strength of gravity. Geese Fortitude is an unparalleled illustration of the spirit of perseverance. Geese totem shows us the extraordinary gift of determination against countless odds.

Eye on the prize is not a frivolous guidepost. Fortitude is the light in the dark, the transcendent soul's voice, the courageous vision of self-expression. Geese Spirit says we are blessed with this innate virtue of the heart, and guides us to be our exceptional and enduring self.

Geese Spirit
Power Message

Yes, I fly high.
I follow the call of the soul.
There is no denying the voice within
For it is your Divine core, not leading you astray.
LISTEN!
It speaks of elated mountains, of infinite oceans
All dwelling within your being.
LISTEN!
The call is beckoning...
Be firm, be of courage, be aware, stand tall.
Fly on course.
Dwell within the space of purpose
It will not lead you astray at all.

Dream Song to Perseverance

Holy Geese!
I only need see you to know the way.
You are without pain of disbelief
You show me how to stay.
Past courses of rough terrain
You travel on, to the point of your gain.
Your grace of being lights the way.
I bow to your inner courage
And know I am not led astray.

Thank you, O Geese Fortitude
For your great Gift of Perseverance

Cloud Dreams

Gift of Inspiration

*Divine inspiration is the birthright
of every human being.
Insights come to and through you.
Ideas are God saying hello.*

Neale Donald Walsch

Geese is one with drifting Cloud in the sky. Cloud offers the opportunity to dream! Daydreaming belongs to the creators of life. It is the quintessential form of inspiration that creates worlds. When one sets their vision on the movement and substance of Cloud, dreams may begin to crystalize. Cloud Dreams drifts one's mental attention to the possibility of all things.

Einstein professed, "Imagination is more important than knowledge." Everything which has ever manifested began with a dream. And the dream began with inspiration.

Be it a cake, a graph, a song, a poem, a building, a garden, a city—the mechanics of the dream begin with the gift of inspiration. From the depth of our being lie open doors into the infinite field of possibility.

Cloud Dreams beckon us to take time out. To let the mind flow within the whirling momentum of creation. To become a part of All That Is. We are all connected to this power source—the spark of consciousness—from whence we came.

It begins with an uncluttered mind, set free by Cloud Spirit. Set your sights on the natural flow of inspired dreaming—daydreaming. Nourish thoughts and feelings of expression of self. They come drifting through consciousness from within. Cloud Dreams are an intrinsic part of self, designed to embrace and enhance evolution. Gaze out your window. Lie in a field. And watch Cloud roll by.

Cloud Spirit Power Message

My power rests within the flow
And so, there you may go.
It is a process of enlightenment
Touching Divine Source within.
Your gift is inspiration.
To and through you, I come and go.
Listen to the words upon your soul.
They will lead you to what you know.
Let go restrictions and challenges
Just see them stream in the dream.

Dream Song to Inspiration

Great Cloud upon my soul!
I see your essence drift and flow
Opening space between all I know.
Linear thoughts come and go
And then you open a dream
To be more.
And follow it I will go.
In a graceful space between fixed thoughts
Offering me infinite visions to be more than I know.

Thank you, O Cloud Dreams
For your great Gift of Inspiration

Celestial Snowflake

Gift Of Diversity

*In 'The Snowflake Like No Other'
the rainbow snowflake, Dazzler reveals
the uniqueness of every living thing.*

Adele Helen Terzis

Great Cloud creates Celestial Snowflake. Billions of crystalized water vapors form infinitely singular Snowflake. Vast uniqueness flourishes in the cosmos.

It is time to recognize the beauty of all things, of all beings, and honor divine diversity. Snowflake is an exquisite example.

Celestial Snowflake begins by forming into a hexagon and grows larger as branches sprout from its six corners. Tumbling through the clouds through varying temperatures and humidity, each change makes Snowflake's arms a bit different. The exact shape of the final crystal is determined by the specific path it traversed. Snowflake's arms all experience the same journey, so they grow in synchrony. And since no two crystals follow the exact path through the clouds, no two look alike.

And so it is with humanity. Through our individual journeys, we form unique characteristics and personalities. We are all great gifts to life. There is something you offer that no one can give in the exact same way. Divine diversity!

It is time to bless ourselves and others for our unique contributions to evolution. They may seem trivial or unnoticed, but they are exceptional. We are all shaped by the choices made through experience. Let us make decisions that support our unique beneficial abilities. Let us endow our greatest gifts to enhance All That Is. This is the reason for divine diversity. Embrace your Celestial Snowflake within.

Snowflake Spirit Power Message

Yes, I flow! I glide into life.
And as I travel through the changes of time
I become beautiful.
I share my exquisite uniqueness with the world.
This is a path of purpose for all.
You may decide, with each taken breath
To build your beauty, rather than fall.
You can decide to grow as you go.
For you are one within all
And glory is your call.

Dream Song to Diversity

Sweet Snowflake, I see you drift.
In all your beauty, there is no flaw.
And I can grow to be my best
In what is my gift to all.
You show me the way to go.
Life unfolds in myriad ways
And my offerings are treasures
To enrich every day.

Thank you, O Celestial Snowflake
For your great Gift of Diversity

Rain Rhythm

Gift of Cycles

> *I am a being of Heaven and Earth*
> *of thunder and lightning,*
> *of rain and wind, of the galaxies.*
>
> Eden Ahbez

Snowflake may change form into the birth of Rain. "Rain, rain, go away; come again another day." No, Rain Rhythm is here to stay. And blessed are we. For without precious Rain, the beauty of life as we know it would not exist.

As we journey through time, intricate patterns are at play. They are progressions of evolution, unifying events gracefully flowing and holding all together.

Rain Rhythm stabilizes and nourishes creation. Earth seasons remind us of the power of progression through the structure of order. Without the gift of cycles, we would not be. Creation exists in a perpetual cycle through a cohesive system of order. Rain Rhythm shows the transcendent value of succession.

Each of us experiences many cycles. Some we consciously adopt to maintain particular paths, and some are drawn to us through our spirit of being. All serve a higher purpose of personal evolution, consciously known or not.

Although Rain Rhythm may fall hard at times, there is divine purpose. Know that life's purpose is to smooth itself out through the living of it. Choice does not always come into play but, rather, a flowing with any experience that comes our way.

Although the going may get tough, know the gift of cycles moves within an eternal celestial wheel, wielding our personal paths into a course of sacredness. Know we are guided by the Great Mystery. Aspire to faith during the downfalls. And rise up during the blessing of the rainbow showers.

Rain Spirit
Power Message

I consecrate life.
I shower with joy and pain
But it never stays the same.
This is earth life you are here to gain
In the practice of humanity and divinity, embraced.
The sprinkling and the downfall are all the same
In the eyes of Spirit.
For they dwell within the flow of eternity.
So, let not your lighthearted dances
And heavy troubles stagnate you
For they are all within the cycle of life.

Dream Song to Cycles

O Rain Rhythm, you come and go as my constant friend.
You teach me the power of the universe
In the tempo of your eternal cycles.
It is here where all life merges, in perfect measure.
Your healing mist and beating storm equally
Guide my constant path.
In the balance I aspire to grow.

Thank you, O Rain Rhythm
For your great Gift of Cycles

Resplendent Rainbow

Gift of Light

My teacher asked my favorite color...
I said, 'Rainbow'.

Saket Assertive

After Rain showers, the symbolic herald of a new day comes with Rainbow. As a visual meteorological phenomenon, Rainbow shimmers in the sky in a miraculous kaleidoscope of colored jewels. Resplendent Rainbow is a continuous spectrum of approximately one hundred detectable hues, with the seven primary colors being prominent.

Rainbow is caused by the marriage of atmospheric water and sunlight. As the light curves, it appears as a reflected spectrum of color in the sky. Iridescent Rainbow blesses us with this communion in a magickal display of shimmering colors.

Delighting us since time began, this chromatic marvel sparks the mind of man to heights of wonder and illumination. Rainbow totem reminds us of the presence of light after darkness.

Rainbow Spirit shines after a storm. When Rainbow's light brightens the sky, it is a balance of energies united in an arc of perfect beauty. Rainbow encourages us to see all the colors of life, knowing light will shine through them all.

This is the message of the eternal harmony of All That Is. Within the earthly drama of darkness, light will surely appear in all its glory, through many colorful experiences. Iridescent Rainbow says, "Do not give up, for the light cometh!"

Rainbow Spirit Power Message

I am the Light of Creation.
All facets lie within me.
Together in all color, a perfect blend of harmony.
I am a unification of energy
Coming into fruition.
Allow life to go, and light will flow.
This is how to live.
Allow honor to bless your path
Through every experience.
You are growing within the spectrum of Spirit
Whose one color is an infusion of love.
There is no separation, you see
All honor must be given thee.
This is how to love.
In a perfect blending of your light
Your colors in harmony.
I enlighten thee.

Dream Song to Light

O Sacred Rainbow
You show me the way
Of non-separation
Only the light of day.
Shining in alignment with you
I feel a harmony so true.
You alight my way.
It is here where life is best lived
In honor of all paths.
I look to you, O Rainbow Spirit
To brighten my soul
Balance my heart
And enlighten my way.
Allow me to give my light
To others every day.

Thank you, O Resplendent Rainbow
For your great Gift of Light

Sovereign Sun

Gift of Benediction

Even after all this time,
the Sun never says to the earth,
'You owe me.'
Look what happens with a love like that—
it lights the whole world.

Hafiz

Beauteous Rainbow receives vitality from Sun's glow. Sun Power! Sovereign Sun, enthroned in the center of our solar system, composes about 99.86 percent *en masse* of our celestial network. Humanity has a minute idea of what this means. It is no wonder cultures and religions throughout time revered this life-giving planet as a powerful deity.

Sovereign Sun is a living being bestowing endless gifts to all it touches. Sunlight has been known to cure depression, improve brain function, promote eye health, heal skin disorders, reduce risk of Type 2 diabetes, boosts immunity, prevents vitamin D deficiency, reduces cancer risks, and lowers high blood pressure. Sun power increases serotonin for well-being and weight loss, improves sleep, enhances bone health, protects against inflammation, assists muscle health, and reduces heart disease. Research also indicates exposure to sunlight reduces Alzheimer's symptoms. And these are just health benefits!

Sovereign Sun is a potent healing elixir. Our world, and earth beings could not flourish without it. The gift of benediction nourishes all living things, which in turn provides life-affirming nutrients to each other through the food-chain.

May we embrace and honor this great entity. We have not begun to realize Sun's benevolent, miraculous benefits, its divine benediction, and the sacred purpose and blessing of organic nuclear energy.

Sun Spirit Power Message

I am a Sacred Seed of Life
And shine upon you.
My light is your light.
We share this sacred bond.
As I give to the world
So may you also.
For at our power core
We are Divine Life.
You are infused with mine
And I, yours.
We bless and return to each other.
This is our power together.

Dream Song to Benediction

O Sovereign Sun!
How you bless All That Is.
It is your gift of giving
The pure essence of you.
You give who you are
In a Divine healing way.
Your core is my core.
Our light shineth together.
I can never deny your light within
For as you warm me with your love
I am infused.

Thank you, O Sovereign Sun
For your great Gift of Benediction

Radiant Fire

Gift of Passion

> *Feelings or emotions are the universal language and are to be honored. They are the authentic expression of who you are at your deepest place.*
>
> Judith Wright

Radiant Fire is bestowed upon us by Sun's brilliant energy. It is life itself, a creative expression of collective consciousness. Fire is a potent element that sparks birth. Fire is power is energy. Energy is passion. Passion creates worlds!

The wise use of passion directs us to creative manifestation. Our gift of passion can grow exponentially and nourish evolution. Radiant Fire is here to remind us of our divine spark of expression within.

Emotions arise to assist in personal growth. They are the heart and soul speaking. No matter what feelings arise, we should always honor them. Our task is to infuse them with love. When emotions are infused with love, they radiate outward and bless All That Is. Moving with positive passion through challenges creates a living wave of altruistic vitality. This beneficial force unifies and blesses the whole of creation.

Aspiring to live in this benevolent way, *Six Power Principles of Creation* come into play: Passion, Path, Perseverance, Positive Thinking, Prayer, and Peace. When combined, these aspects of manifestation expand the life-sustaining energies of the universe. In this way, one simple act of love may create worlds.

Fire Spirit Power Message

Yes, I am growing. Yes, I am anointing.
It is *you* who I come to bless.
For your fire within is the lifeblood of creation.
We have come together to birth life, *ad infinitum*.
This natural labor is in your hands
A gift of your Divine Passion.
Let it fire you up!
Be not a naysayer, but a consecrator.
Blessed Be are thee to me.

Dream Song to Passion

O Fire within
Bless me with your Divine Radiance.
Let me shine your luminous life!
I endeavor to use passion in its highest light.
To bless, and heal, and guide
To gather with others and unite in the dream
In the infinite creation of the beauty of life.

Thank you, O Radiant Fire,
For your great Gift of Passion

Morning Glory

Gift of Becoming

> *There was never a night or a problem that could defeat sunrise.*
>
> Bernard Williams

The Fire of the Morning alights a new day. As the world awakens, rebirth has sprung. The message is loud and clear—Morning has risen.

Morning Glory is symbolic of a fresh start, an overturn of the past, a moving forward into a *new now*. It is here where we may look up at the opening sky and proclaim, *I become anew*.

Sun has not slipped away during the evening, but merely moved to make space for inner reflection during Moonglow. And now, as Moon descends, Morning trumpets an embrace of conscious beginning.

"A brand-new day" is a common term representing a choice of change through the evolution of being. We may all take up this rally for personal rebirth anytime we desire.

Morning Glory may wipe the proverbial self-slate clean and completely overhaul one's perceptions. Or Morning may, through soft light rays, absorb into our being and awaken desires for growth. Either way, the gift of becoming is at hand.

Morning Glory is a time to celebrate and cherish the progressing path of our journey. It is a time to honor what has been and enfold new levels of awareness within. We are all on a path of self-discovery. Morning brightens the way with birdsong, and gentle light turning into a bold rosy display. Flowers open with Morning's warm smile. We rub sleepiness from our eyes and see light streaming. Life is becoming! Morning Glory's gift is a personal blessing of love from above.

Morning Spirit Power Message

O, I shine on thee!
I alight your flame within to see.
From the cocoon of your darkness
I warm your body to rise again.
Come, follow my way.
Without my glory you would never see another day.
So come forth from the night
And shine your own light.
You are One with me.

MESSAGES FROM THE CONSCIOUSNESS OF OUR WORLD

Dream Song to Becoming

Blessed Be, Morning Glory!
You wake me up from dreams of old.
I feel your light upon my soul.
You gently, boldly bid me hello
That I may awake anew and grow.
Blessed Be, O Morning song!
You entice me to move on
Becoming the best of me.

Thank you, O Morning Glory
For your great Gift of Becoming

Twilight Time

Gift of Connection

In the twilight, it was a vision of power.

Upton Sinclair

As Morning slowly fades, Twilight Time heralds a shift of consciousness. Twilight—that magickal space of a melding of worlds. A coalescence of physical and mystical. A slowing of the corporal senses heightened by preternatural inclinations. A perfect blend of human and Spirit emerges whether we are aware or not.

Twilight Time. The veil thins between the visible and invisible, and a profound reunion takes place. It is here, when the light of day descends, and night arises. When etheric beings on the other side emerge perceptive. It is here where the gift of connection may be keenly experienced. The connection of all beings.

Betwixt and between is the magick of Twilight Time. *Merriam-Webster Dictionary* describes betwixt and between as "in a midway position: neither one thing nor the other." This is the transcendent feeling one may experience within the conscious energy of Twilight. It is a sublime state of being one with another world.

This enchanted world of reality exists, and Twilight is a space where we may, as humans, touch the soul of harmonious union with the unseen. It is akin to feeling vitally alive. It is an enlightenment of the spiritual seed of connection within self, with all life.

Twilight Time is a period of great potential. We may consciously use its energy as a way to empower self through the inherent divine relationship with creation. The mundane may interlude with the spiritual in a most dynamic way. You may even feel sparkling skin stars upon your being!

Twilight Spirit Power Message

Yes, I am alive!
I come to share all the glories of One.
Here you stand, on this rotating earth
And think it is all you can feel?
Nay, eternity is before you.
In the mist of Twilight
I bring you together with your Self.
Infinite Spirit is before you.
The veil has been cast; connection is at hand.
I am that sacred space between day and night
When all may be revealed.
Life unseen dances before you.
Open your heart and head, Dear Ones
Connection is at hand.

Dream Song to Connection

Yes, I hear you, O shimmering Twilight!
I hear your siren-song calling
Open, receive, be, commune.
All life is before me
The dream of oneness is at hand.
All beings unite within you.
I embrace your day into night
And know that all is revealed.
The power of sacred union is bestowed.

Thank you, O Twilight Time
For your great Gift of Connection

Eternal Eventide

Gift of Peace

*Sometimes I go about in pity for myself
and all the while a great wind
carries me across the sky.*

Ancient Ojiwa Proverb

Born of twinkling Twilight, sacred Eventide reveals. *The cosmos is alive.* The heavens speak of the order of all things. Within this realm, peace is bestowed. It is the infinite alignment of creation—as above, so below. It is the realization of the great cosmic flow that we may know. In this timeless space, we may let the mundane go. Let it flow into the black of the night to be blessed by the divine celestial.

There is no mystery here. It is written in the stars. Watch the skies and be exalted. We look upon the vast firmament with wonder and aspire to guess. But, look deeper, look longer. You will be drawn into the secret, and peace will come to rest. It is the intention of all things.

Yes, there is chaos and the temporary crumbling of all that we know. We wonder at the state of the world. We want peace. But brilliant stars burst forth in fiery birth and shine luminous in the eon sky. And so it may be with thee.

"But if a man would be alone, let him look at the stars. One might think the atmosphere was made transparent with this design, to give man, in the heavenly bodies, the perpetual presence of the sublime," intuits Ralph Waldo Emerson

So, look upon life with the peace of understanding. Even as what appears chaotic is creating beauty. Be one with the expanse of the stellar sky. Lay thyself down under the heavens and absorb the eternal. All is well in the cosmos. You have your place in the world.

Eventide Spirit Power Message

I am the fire and water of life.
I shine for you to see—for you to be.
It is by my light and darkness that you may know
That you will grow.
For I tell you of the dream.
It is all within peace where chaos dwells.
It is the soul of the Divine Plan.
From the starry distance you see silence
Wherein the astral heart manifests
Exploding birth!
And so it is, the harmonic vision of peace prevails.

Dream Song to Peace

Sacred Eventide, I beseech unto thee
I seek the quiet rest of your soul.
I see you in beautiful harmony
Your infinite starry expanse
And wonder at this place of being in the All.
Your tranquility is in perpetual motion
Your breath of fire creating worlds.
Yet I feel your serene energy blessing me forth
In the creation and awakening of peace.

Thank you, O Eternal Eventide
For your great Gift of Peace

Miraculous Moonglow

Gift of Illumination

*I am in love with the moon
with the light shining
out of its soul.*

Sanober Khan

Through the dark passage of Eventide births the Queen of the Night—Miraculous Moon. Moon's enchanted glow is hypnotic, and as our closest planetary neighbor, its magnetic emanations draw on the intimate bodies of earth and all beings.

In the deepest dark of the night, Moon shines on, lighting the pilgrim's way and brightening the path with a luminous soul. Within Moon's effervescent glow, we stand in wonder, infused with radiance.

What is the allure and miracle of Moonglow? It is the reflection and power of Sovereign Sun, the giver of life. Moon generously absorbs this energy and benevolently shares it with the world, shining its healing gift on all.

Miraculous Moon's gift is illumination. In the dark, there is forever a spark of holy light. It is the power of imminent spiritual insight. A sacred knowledge that upholds the truth of self—the sovereignty within.

We perpetually have the choice to reflect this blessed power. It is our divine right and inheritance. Amidst the dark, illumination is at hand through one thought of love at a time.

Moon's way is a path of the heart. It is the faith of the eternal life-giving Sun. It is the wisdom of humanity's soul come to light. It is the empowerment of love's radiance shining in the night. Stand in immaculate Moonglow and bathe in heavenly consciousness.

Moonglow Spirit Power Message

O Holy Ones, see the light!
You are a part of all that shines.
You are a part of all Divine.
Do not waste your tears of pain.
See all the love there is to gain.
It is your power, you see
Your sacred right to be one with me.
For as you shine above, your soul will rise
And meet the kingdom within.
Blessed Be your Spirit, Blessed Be thee.

Dream Song to Illumination

Beauteous Moonglow, you open me, I can see!
For in your hallowed light, I become me.
I feel the strength of your Spirit within
And know it is One, and all of me again.
I feel your heavenly essence absorb into me
Filling me with an awareness of reality.
I bless your radiant being for showing the way.
Through the darkness I go
and move into the light of day.

Thank you, O Miraculous Moonglow
For your great Gift of Illumination

Earth Blessing

Gift of Devotion

I am so absorbed in the wonder of earth and the life upon it that I cannot think of heaven and angels.

Pearl S. Buck

Moon shines upon our blessed world, our sacred fertile Mother. Sustaining us since the beginning of time, earth is the holy maternal. Every step we take, every breath we make is part of her Spirit.

We are eternally embraced in Gaia's living, loving arms. Earth is our paradise found. From the deepest ocean depths to the highest mountain peak, our world emanates infinite blessings, nourishing unconditionally. This gift of devotion is the essence of her supreme heart.

As we walk upon her body, we may consciously absorb her beautiful benediction. It is a cleansing of adverse ions and a refueling of life-energy vibrations of the highest order.

In the conscious state, we allow ourselves to open more fully to receive. Any mindful connection with the purity of Mother Earth—via plant, mineral, air, or water—is a virtuous act of love and honor. It is the greatest value to commune with nature, as it opens pure channels of divine intervention for unification. What transpires is communion with the soul of life.

Earth Blessing sings the song of living. Ever growing, ever changing in eternal evolution. Moment by moment, Gaia supports our sacred journey of being. With her companion the Sun, Gaia bestows the greatest gift to the flowering of creation—devotion.

Earth Spirit Power Message

I nurture your body in the purity of love
For as you walk upon my soil, I am one with you.
Our hearts beat as One
For our intimacy is like no other.
Yet you mistreat me with harsh undertakings
And distance yourself from my love.
But, I forever feed your soil
For I am ground for your growth.
The day will come when we shall rejoice as One
And a holy day that shall be, for all eternity!
So, I proclaim:
Look to my body as a sacred vessel of your heart
Where love can reign and conquer discontent.
For as you believe in me, so shall we be together.
My blessings are always upon you, my children.

Dream Song to Devotion

Glory Earth, my heart and soul
Your grace is beyond compare.
For in your giving, we bountifully grow.
There would be no "we" without your body
this I know.
Praise life, every living thing
For in this thriving we are nourished to grow.
May my senses ever be aware
Of your great sacred care
For you are my Holy Mother always embracing me
Your loving child.

Thank you, O Earth Blessing
For your great Gift of Devotion

Drum Chant

Gift of Spirit Dance

Everything in the universe has rhythm.
Everything dances.

Maya Angelou

Through the body of Gaia sings a creative cosmic prayer—the unified heartbeat of creation. Drum Chant beats with this pulsating divine dance.

The sacredness and vitality of Drum has been expressed since the beginning of time. Sloth's algae garden also benefits many insects who obtain shelter in its fur – even birds harmlessly nibble on the nutritious ecosystem growing on this sweet mammal's lush coat.

Although Drum is not typically considered a natural being by modern society, its essence is composed of nature's corporeal and spiritual components. Indigenous nations and intuitive modern man have always honored Drum as a living being. Drum's organic Spirit sings in harmony with the core of Mother Earth and the celestial Music of the Spheres. The collective voice of Drum Chant is the most primordial tribal world beat—the heart and rhythm of life energies pulsating throughout the cosmos.

Native cultures traditionally evoked Drum's mystical power to enrich tribal councils and pow-wows. Drum Chant established shamanic distinction, was used as a trance path to enrich and heal soul journeys and enhanced other ritualized and religious customs. Much of this spiritual practice continues to be honored and performed in modern sacred ceremony and celebration today.

Recently, an expanded interest in the benefits of drumming has been borrowed from past times as a valuable tool for personal expression and social connection. Increasing within world communities, this ancient art has come full-circle as a pathway to spiritual, emotional, and physical integration and well-being.

Drum Chant offers the great gift of Spirit Dance. As we commune on a deep level with ourselves and all beings through its voice, it lifts us ever-upward into the divine dance of cosmic unity.

Drum Spirit
Power Message

I am Spirit of Drum
And we are the Voice of One.
I call you from far away
From the heart of sacred earth.
Hear me calling you, calling you
The Beat of One
Into the depths of Mother Earth
Mingling with Father Sky
Your Spirit flying high!
Hear me, O daughter, hear me, O son.
Drum Chant, Spirit Dance
As we become the Song of One.

Dream Song to Spirit Dance

Rising from the depths of Source
I dance in Spirit with the beat of Drum.
Heartbeat, Earth beat
Beat as One.
Earth Mother moves through my blood
And I am grounded to fly,
rising up and soaring high.
Drum Chant, Spirit Dance
Beat as One.
We dance, we chant
We move as One.
I am the song of life's soul.
Heartbeat, Earth beat
We are One.
And the beat goes on.

Thank you, O Drum Chant
For your great Gift of Spirit Dance

Human-Kind

Gift of Heart

*What is the heart? It is not human,
and it is not imaginary.
I call it You.*

Rumi

Nature beings walk to the beat of Drum Spirit. Humanity is part of this diverse family, a bountiful species roaming earth. In consciousness, we delight in being a part of Mother's widespread creation. Through all our actions, compassion is prominent within the heart of Human-Kind.

Everywhere we look, sometimes deeply, Human-Kind sets the standards for gentle compassion. It is divinely inherent within our truest nature as we step up with a fullness of heart and bestow goodwill.

Throughout our day, random acts of kindness prevail across the world. We may know little of these collective deeds, because modern media does not highlight their blessings, but their light shines through the aethers[11] of our earth plane and beyond. Infinite, abundant blessings prevail. Throughout our day, these beautiful benedictions of loving kindness may be absorbed within. It just takes an opening of the heart to receive. Breathe and receive.

We each possess the Sacred Heart within. A thought, a word, an act of compassion works miracles across the land. We are powerful divine beings of love. We touch hearts, we heal, we consecrate. It is the greatest gift of time, the greatest gift of Human-Kind. Let us do it for each other; let us do it for all others; let us do it for life.

---

11   Refer to footnote on page 49.

Human-Kind Spirit Power Message

I, we, are beautiful blessings.
An open heart is the true path of living.
There is no other reason to survive.
Giving love makes us truly alive.
It is our right, it is our duty
The elixir of life.
Sit with this, BE THIS!
It is time to take the reins of your sacred power.
Human-Kind Spirit is needed every hour.

Dream Song to Heart

I rest in my heart.
I know of its mission.
There is only one way to go
This, in my soul, I truly know.
Beautiful heart, expand your love!
Sing the beating song within.
For all else is not worth the notes
Unless love be its call.
Dearest Human-Kind, take hands
And lead each other into the Promised Land.

Thank you, O Human-Kind
For your great Gift of Heart

*I turn to the Great Spirit's book
which is the whole of creation.
You can read a big part of that book
if you study nature.
You know, if you take all your books,
lay them out under the sun,
and let the snow and rain and insects
work on them for a while, there will be nothing left.
But the Great Spirit has provided you and me
with an opportunity for study in nature's university,
the forests, the rivers, the mountains,
and the animals which include us.*

                      Walking Buffalo

MESSAGES FROM THE CONSCIOUSNESS OF OUR WORLD

Passage Three

THE JOURNEY NEVER ENDS
Life Everlasting

EarthLight's Healing Power
Eternal Gift of Transformation

When the powers of nature are the focus of your awareness and your thoughts, you come near to spirit, near to the source of all life. This is why most people love to walk in the woods or by the sea: they come close to the original source, and it is healing just to be in its presence. It cleanses you, brings peace of mind, touches your heart, and brings you home to your soul.

Chris Luttichau

EarthLight is the benevolent spirit of our world that can heal all things. How does nature heal? In a myriad of ways, many of which we may be unaware, yet they continue to manifest and nourish. One true way to receive the power of active healing is through communion. And this begins with *intimacy.*

Through the beautiful act of conscious intimacy, we honor and heal each other. What is intimacy? It is an opening of heart—a seeing through the eyes of love. It is the soul of gratitude, respect, and a giving from within. It is a knowing of the holy gifts of our Great Mother.

From intimacy with Gaia's body, we touch her soul. We remember she is a source of our life. There is no thriving without her. Intimacy begets true communion, and communion opens the heart to receive her blessings. Then a beautiful healing has begun.

Go back to the sacred ways of the indigenous and connect with your power of love within. A wellspring of life will open before you. It will be a return home.

EarthLight Stewardship
A Return Home

Nature is not a place to visit. It is home.

Gary Snyder

Nature has presented herself in such a way that we cannot deny her wisdom, power, beauty, and voice any longer. She is our Sacred Mother.

When we truly see our world, we look with heart-eyes. Our world is beyond time and space yet contains it. Nature is the song, the dance of eternity. Nature is a different being, yet we are of her one body—the whole of creation.

Gaia is here to stay as long as she desires. Humanity may temporarily destruct part of her, but that is just a step toward our own sad demise. In essence it is our lives we should be concerned about. As a species who desires to remain alive, without nature's flourishing gifts, we are in dire peril. And if we self-destruct, she will continue to thrive—replenish, sustain, and nurture herself. How is this possible? Because within Gaia's core dwells an eternal *love and nourishment of creation*. Part of humanity lacks this inherent heart-value.

Why don't we consciously decide to stay on earth and enjoy her life-giving fruits? It begins with the respect of active stewardship, with an aspiration to embrace, with deep gratitude, earth's divine source of unconditional love—the kind of love that forever blesses as her great gifts continue to shower upon us.

Life's Saving Grace
How Blessed Thou Art

Nature is full of paradox, in that as you seek contact with what you consider a lower form of life, you in fact contact a more universal being.

Dorothy Maclean

Every star, every breeze, every worm is an expression of Spirit. Every being of nature, including humanity, is a potential expression of the power of love. Love is life's saving grace. It is through our harmony together that we create peace and beauty—the divine qualities that bless and nourish life.

"You cannot get through a single day without having an impact on the world around you. What you do makes a difference, and you have to decide what kind of difference you want to make," intuits Jane Goodall.

It is time… time to rise to this awareness, lest we lose each other. Unless we realize our vital connection to all life forms, we will lose an integral part of ourselves.

Being whole means expressing and living in unity through life-affirming thought, word, and deed. This higher consciousness will create heaven on earth. It is being in sacred kinship with all beings. It is a harmonic balance with all expressions of consciousness. This is the true path to giving and receiving life's abundant blessings.

Abracadabra is an Aramaic phrase literally meaning "I will create as I speak." Let us sing with the song of the cosmos and create life!

Blessed Be Nature, You, and Me

Epilogue

Our truest nature to fully connect, heal, and grow is to be mirrored by something that reflects our full essence. I believe the natural world is that ideal mirror.

Regina M Powers

Dear Friends,

Thank you for journeying with me through these pages into the heart of nature.

As you move forward in life, it is my wish that you embrace the natural world as your Mother, Father, Sister, Brother, Friend, Lover—Soul. Our connection is without separation. Our kinship of energy is forever entwined. We are one miraculous intimate body of being amidst divine diversity.

Enfolded in the infinite vitality of the universe we are bonded through the living heart of love. It is here, in this transcendent space of being, where all wrongs are righted, where the peace that passeth all understanding dwells.

Bless you and bless all others as we continue our glorious part in the eternal flow of life. As ancient sage Rumi expressed so eloquently, "Love is the bridge between you and everything."

In Lak'ech Ala K'in ~ *I am another you,*

Diana

Nature Beings Index

Ant ~ Gift of Ingenuity	160
Bat ~ Gift of Transcendence	44
Bear ~ Gift of Dreamtime	64
Bird ~ Gift of Hope and Glory	220
Bovine ~ Gift of Generosity	172
Bunny ~ Gift of Providence	184
Butterfly ~ Gift of Serendipity	132
Cave ~ Gift of Inner Beauty	40
Chipmunk ~ Gift of Conservation	216
Cloud ~ Gift of Inspiration	308
Crow ~ Gift of Vigilance	116
Dandelion ~ Gift of Adaptation	136
Dog ~ Gift of Joy	284
Dolphin ~ Gift of Magick	296
Dragonfly ~ Gift of Choice	112
Drum ~ Gift of Spirit Dance	352
Dunes ~ Gift of Change	264
Eagle ~ Gift of Vision	52
Earth ~ Gift of Devotion	348
Elephant ~ Gift of Compassion	248
Equine ~ Gift of Freedom	92
Eventide ~ Gift of Peace	340
Falls ~ Gift of Wonder	56
Fawn ~ Gift of Innocence	88
Fern ~ Gift of Birth	80
Fire ~ Gift of Passion	328
Flora ~ Gift of Sensuality	128
Forest ~ Gift of Strength	72
Frog ~ Gift of Transmutation	104
Fuchsia ~ Gift of Abundance	224
Garden Gate ~ Gift of Restoration	192
Geese ~ Gift of Perseverance	304
Goat ~ Gift of Curiosity	168
Harvest ~ Gift of Well-Being	196
Honeybee ~ Gift of Integrity	208

Human-Kind ~ Gift of Heart	356
Iguana ~ Gift of Strategy	256
Kitty ~ Gift of Knowing Now	212
Ladybug ~ Gift of Friendship	140
Lake ~ Gift of Reflection	240
Lavender ~ Gift of Attraction	200
Lotus ~ Gift of Resurrection	236
Meadow ~ Gift of Harmony	120
Moonglow ~ Gift of Illumination	344
Morning ~ Gift of Becoming	332
Moss ~ Gift of Survival	76
Mountain ~ Gift of Solitude	36
Octopus ~ Gift of Wit	276
Owl ~ Gift of Mystery	68
Palm ~ Gift of Relaxation	268
Pampas ~ Gift of Grace	288
Peacock ~ Gift of Celebration	244
Pig ~ Gift of Affection	176
Prana ~ Gift of Life	232
Quail ~ Gift of Intention	164
Queen Anne's Lace ~ Gift of Elegance	292
Rain ~ Gift of Cycles	316
Rainbow ~ Gift of Light	320
Raspberry ~ Gift of Manifestation	144
River ~ Gift of Adventure	96
Rooster ~ Gift of Expression	188
Rose ~ Gift of Love	228
Sea ~ Gift of Unity	272
Seagull ~ Gift of Ascension	280
Seed ~ Gift of Legacy	148
Sheep ~ Gift of Whimsy	180
Silent Sound ~ Gift of Inner Music	84
Sloth ~ Gift of Purpose	252
Snake ~ Gift of Liberation	260
Snowflake ~ Gift of Divine Diversity	312
Soil ~ Gift of Fertility	152
Spring ~ Gift of Expansion	124

Stone ~ Gift of Conscious Living 100
Stream ~ Gift of Spontaneity 60
Sun ~ Gift of Benediction 324
Sunflower ~ Gift of Energy 204
Turtle ~ Gift of Inner Clock 108
Twilight ~ Gift of Connection 336
Whale ~ Gift of Wisdom 300
Wolf ~ Gift of Communion 48
Worm ~ Gift of Alchemy 156

Nature's Gift Index

Abundance ~ Hummer Fuchsia	224
Adaptation ~ Dainty Dandelion	136
Adventure ~ Rolling River	96
Affection ~ Playful Pig	176
Alchemy ~ Worm Wizard	156
Ascension ~ Soaring Seagull	280
Attraction ~ Lovely Lavender	200
Becoming ~ Morning Glory	332
Benediction ~ Sovereign Sun	324
Birth ~ Furling Fern	80
Celebration ~ Peacock Pleasure	244
Change ~ Shifting Dunes	264
Choice ~ Daring Dragonfly	112
Communion ~ Wolf Song	48
Compassion ~ Endearing Elephant	248
Connection ~ Twilight Time	336
Conscious Living ~ Simple Stone	100
Conservation ~ Chipmunk Patrol	216
Curiosity ~ Gregarious Goat	168
Cycles ~ Rain Rhythm	316
Devotion ~ Earth Blessing	348
Diversity ~ Celestial Snowflake	312
Dreamtime ~ Bear Bed	64
Elegance ~ Queen Anne's Lace	292
Energy ~ Sunflower Power	204
Expansion ~ Heavenly Spring	124
Expression ~ Rousing Rooster	188
Fertility ~ Miracle Soil	152
Freedom ~ Sublime Equine	92
Friendship ~ Lucky Ladybug	140
Gentleness ~ Beautiful Bovine	172
Grace ~ Peaceful Pampas	288
Harmony ~ Meandering Meadow	120
Heart ~ Human-Kind	356
Hope and Glory ~ Bird Psalm	220

Illumination ~ Miraculous Moonglow	334
Ingenuity ~ Amazing Ant	160
Inner Beauty ~ Jeweled Cave	40
Inner Clock ~ Turtle Time	108
Inner Music ~ Silent Sound	84
Innocence ~ Fair Fawn	88
Inspiration ~ Cloud Dreams	308
Integrity ~ Honeybee Honor	208
Intention ~ Captain Quail	164
Joy ~ Darling Dog	284
Knowing Now ~ Buddha Kitty	212
Knowledge ~ Whale Wisdom	300
Legacy ~ Sentient Seed	148
Liberation ~ Shaman Snake	260
Life ~ Sacred Prana	232
Light ~ Resplendent Rainbow	320
Love ~ Rose Divine	228
Magick ~ Dolphin Dance	296
Manifestation ~ Ravishing Raspberry	144
Mystery ~ Owl Mantra	68
Passion ~ Radiant Fire	328
Peace ~ Eternal Eventide	340
Perseverance ~ Geese Fortitude	304
Providence ~ Bountiful Bunny	184
Purpose ~ Sage Sloth	252
Reflection ~ Luminous Lake	240
Relaxation ~ Calming Palm	268
Restoration ~ Garden Gate	192
Resurrection ~ Holy Lotus	236
Sensuality ~ Flora Aurora	128
Serendipity ~ Brilliant Butterfly	132
Solitude ~ Mountain Majesty	36
Spirit Dance ~ Drum Chant	352
Spontaneity ~ Sparkling Stream	60
Strategy ~ Ancient Iguana	256
Strength ~ Forest Cathedral	72
Survival ~ Miracle Moss	76

Transcendence ~ Numinous Bat	44
Transmutation ~ Frog Prince	104
Unity ~ Sea Mandala	272
Vigilance ~ King Crow	116
Vision ~ Regal Eagle	52
Well-Being ~ Healing Harvest	196
Whimsy ~ Sweet Sheep	180
Wit ~ Trickster Octopus	276
Wonder ~ Enchanted Falls	56

Inspirational Quotes and Poetry

Beauty before me
Beauty behind me
Beauty all around me

Navajo Prayer of Gratitude

My soul can find no staircase to Heaven
unless it be through Earth's loveliness.

Michelangelo

The goal of life is to make your heartbeat
match the beat of the universe.
To match your nature with Nature.

Joseph Campbell

Forget not that the earth delights
to feel your bare feet
And the winds long to play with your hair.

Kahlil Gibran

When we recognize the virtues, the talent,
the beauty of Mother Earth,
something is born in us,
some kind of connection;
love is born.

Thich Nhat Hanh

I hear the voice
of every creature and plant
Every word and sun and galaxy
Singing the Beloved's name.

    Hafiz

The force that through the green fuse
drives the flower drives my green age....
the force that drives the water through the rocks
drives my red blood...

    Dylan Thomas

The magic begins in you. Feel your own energy, and realize similar energy exists within the earth, stones, plants, water, wind, fire, colours, and animals.

    Scott Cunningham

Remember you are WATER
Cry. Cleanse. Flow. Let It Go.
Remember you are FIRE
Burn. Tame. Adapt. Ignite.
Remember you are AIR
Observe. Breathe. Focus. Decide.
Remember you are EARTH
Ground. Build. Produce. Give.
Remember you are SPIRIT
Connect. Listen. Know. Be Still.

    Carrie Love

This body is like the earth.
Our bones are like mountains.
Our belly is like the sea.
Our flesh is like the dust and mud.
The hair that grows on us is like plants, and the skin
from which this hair grows is like arable land,
and the area of our body where hair
does not grow is akin to saline soil.
Our sadness is like darkness and
our laughter like sunlight.
Sleep is brother to death.
Our childhood is like spring,
our youth like summer.
Our maturity is like the autumn,
our old age like the winter of life.
All of our movements are like
the stars moving in the sky.

Shems Friedlander

Our ancestors said to their Mother Earth:
'We are yours'.
Modern Humanity said to Nature, 'You are mine'.
The Green Man has returned as the living face
of the whole earth so that through his mouth
we may say to the universe: we are One.'

Sharon Brubaker

We often forget that we are nature.
Nature is not something separate from us.
So when we say we have lost our connection to nature,
we've really lost our connection to ourselves.

Andy Goldsworthy

Underneath the surface appearance, everything
is not only connected with everything else,
but also with the Source of all life out of which it came.
Even a stone, or more easily a flower or a bird,
could show you the way back to God, to Source,
to yourself. Its essence silently communicates itself
to you and reflects your own essence back to you.

        Eckhart Tolle

People normally cut reality into compartments,
and so are unable to see the interdependence of all
phenomena. To see one in all and all in one
is to break through the great barrier
which narrows one's perceptions of reality.

        Thich Nhat Hanh

If we surrendered to earth's intelligence
We could rise up rooted like trees.

        Rainer Maria Rilke

And this our life exempt from public haunt
finds tongues in trees, books in the running brooks
sermons in stones, and good in everything.

        William Shakespeare

Look deep into Nature
then you will understand everything better.

        Albert Einstein

Nature heals, Nature reveals.

Anonymous

Place your hands into soil to feel grounded.
Wade into water to feel emotionally healed.
Fill your lungs with fresh air to feel mentally clear.
Raise your face to the heat of the sun and connect
with that fire to feel your own immense power.

Victoria Erickson

Climb the mountains and get their good tidings.
Nature's peace will flow into you as sunshine flows
into trees. The winds will blow their own freshness
into you, and the storms their energy, while cares
will drop away from you like the leaves of Autumn.

John Muir

Every now and then we must take a good look
at something not made of human hands.
A mountain, a tree, a star,
or just the turn of a stream.
There will come to you a great wisdom, patience,
and solace. And above all else, the assurance
that you are not alone in the world.
Find relief where the pines flourish,
and the jay still screams.

Sidney Lovett

I remember a hundred lovely lakes,
and recall the fragrant breath of pine
and fir and cedar and poplar trees.
The trail has strung upon it, as upon a thread of silk,
opalescent dawns and saffron sunsets.
It has given me blessed release from care and worry
and the troubled thinking of our modern day.
It has been a return to the primitive and the peaceful.
Whenever the pressure of our complex city life
thins my blood and benumbs my brain,
I seek relief in the trail;
and when I hear the coyote wailing to the yellow dawn,
my cares fall from me – I am happy.

Hamlin Garland

What do shamans do in times of stress?
They talk to the sun, they talk to the earth.
They talk to the spirit of water and the spirit of air.
They talk to the trees and animals.
And they do not pretend they know everything.

Anonymous

There is a place I go
When life gets too static and civilization seems far from civil
It is a place where they all know me and everyone is free
Where I can sit in solitude and feel the earth's energy
Be at peace with everything around me
Where I can hear the voices of animals
A place where I can speak
the secret language of trees.

Emelia

Feathers carry through the wind...
BE SOFT
Do not let the world make you hard
Do not let the pain make you hate
Do not let the bitterness steal your sweetness
Take pride that even though the rest
of the world may disagree ...
You still believe it to be a beautiful place.

Iain Thomas

The old Lakota was wise.
He knew that a man's heart, away from nature, becomes hard;
he knew that lack of respect for growing,
living things soon led to lack of respect for humans, too.
So he kept his children close to nature's softening influence.
Everything was possessed of personality, only differing
from us in form. Knowledge was inherent in all things.
The world was a library and its books were the stones,
leaves, grass, brooks, and the birds and animals that shared,
alike with us, the storms and blessings of earth.
We learned to do what only the student of nature learns,
and that was to feel beauty. We never railed at the storms,
the furious winds, and the biting frosts and snows.
To do so intensified human futility, so whatever came
we adjusted ourselves, by more effort
and energy if necessary, but without complaint.

Sicangu and Oglala Lakota Sioux
Chief Luther Standing Bear

What if our religion was each other?
If our practice was our life?
What if the temple was the earth?
If forests were our church?
If holy water—the rivers, lakes, and oceans?
What if meditation was our relationships?
If the Teacher was life?
If wisdom was knowledge?
If love was the center of our being.

    Ganga White

Every animal has his or her story,
his or her thoughts, daydreams, and interests.
All feel joy and love, pain and fear,
as we now know beyond any shadow of a doubt.
All deserve that the human animal afford them
the respect of being cared for with great consideration
for those interests or left in peace.

    Ingrid Newkirk

There is still a window of time.
Nature can win if we give her a chance.

    Dr. Jane Goodall

It is finished in beauty
It is finished in beauty

    Navaho Night Way Song

Inspirational Books

A Book of Angels ~ Sophie Burnham, Ballantine Books, 1990
A Flower Unfolds ~ Marjorie Musacchio, Sun Sprite Publishing, 2003
A New Earth ~ Eckhart Tolle, Penguin Books, 2005
A Thousand Names for Joy ~ Byron Katie, Harmony Books, 2007
Animal Speak ~ Ted Andrews, Llewellyn Publication, 1993
Autobiography of a Yogi ~ Paramahansa Yogananda, The Philosophical Library, 1946
Be Here Now ~ Ram Dass, Llama Foundation, 1971
Behaving as if the God in all Life Mattered ~ Machaelle Small Wright, Perelandra, Ltd., 1983
Change Your Thoughts – Change Your Life ~ Dr. Wayne W. Dyer, Hay House, Inc., 2007
Dolphin Connection ~ Joan Ocean, Spiral/Dolphin Connection, 1989
Dying to be Me ~ Anita Moorjani, Hay House, Inc., 2012
Enchantment of the Faerie Realm ~ Ted Andrews, Llewellyn Worldwide, Ltd., 1993
Gift from the Sea ~ Anne Morrow Lindbergh, Pantheon Books, 1955
Guided Imagery for Self-Healing ~ Martin Rossman, HJ Kramer, Inc., 2010
In the Presence of Higher Beings: What Dolphins Want You to Know ~ Bobbie Sandoz-Merrill, Chicago Review Press, 2005
Jonathan Livingston Seagull ~ Richard Bach, Macmillan Publishers, 1970
Journey Into Nature ~ Michael Rhoades, HJ Kramer, Inc., 1990
No More To Need ~ Jill Hardin, Xlibris Publishing, 2009
Out on a Limb ~ Shirley MacLaine, Bantam Books, 1983

Phantoms Afoot ~ Mary Summer Rain, Whitford Press, 1989
Power of Flowers ~ Isha Lerner, U.S. Games Systems Inc., 2000
Sacred Journey of the Peaceful Warrior ~ Dan Millman, HJ Kramer, Inc., 1990
Summer with the Leprechauns ~ Tanis Helliwell, Blue Dolphin Publishing, Inc., 1997
Talking to Heaven ~ James Van Praagh, Signet Publishing, 1997
The Ascension Oracle ~ Natalia M Schott, Rose House Publishing, 2011
The Findhorn Garden Story ~ The Findhorn Community, Findhorn Press, 2008
The Four Agreements ~ Don Miguel Ruiz, Amber-Allen Publishing, 1997
The Prophet ~ Kahlil Gibran, Alfred A. Knopf, Inc., 1923
The Quiet Mind ~ White Eagle Publishing Trust, 2008
The Real World of Fairies ~ Dora Van Gelder, Quest Books, 1995
The Secret Life of Plants ~ Peter Tompkins and Christopher Bird, Harper and Row, 1973
The Sense of Wonder ~ Rachael Carson, HarperCollins Publishers, 1965
The Snow Leopard ~ Peter Matthiessen, Viking Press, 1978
The Subject Tonight is Love ~ Hafiz translated by Daniel Ladinsky, Penguin Group, 1996
The Wisdom of Insecurity ~ Alan W. Watts, Pantheon Books, 1951
Walden ~ Henry David Thoreau, Peter Pauper Press, 1888
When Trees Say Nothing ~ Thomas Merton, Sorin Books, 2003
Why Love Heals ~ Dean Shrock, PhD., Likely 1st Edition, 2009

Inspirational Videos

Symphony of Science ~ "We Are All Connected"
melodysheep
Published on Oct 19, 2009
https://www.youtube.com/watch?v=XGK84Poeynk

What Is Hidden From Us
Sustainable Human
Published on Jan 22, 2019
https://www.youtube.com/watch?v=2zko4S5yFnM

How Forests Heal People
Nitin Das
Published on Oct 19, 2016
https://www.youtube.com/watch?v=y-wHq6yY2CI

Fantastic Fungi: The Spirit of Good
Paul Stamets
Published on Jan 23, 2012
Moving Art by Louie Schwartzberg
https://www.youtube.com/watch?v=2wzBPSbTGYM

How Wolves Change Rivers
Sustainable Human
Published on Feb 13, 2014
https://www.youtube.com/watch?v=ysa5OBhXz-Q&t=6s

Speaking to the Water
Uplift
Published on Dec 11, 2017
https://www.youtube.com/watch?v=OeeAMNxuqio

How Whales Changes Climate
Sustainable Human
Published on Nov 15, 2017
https://www.youtube.com/watch?v=rwZR28su0FU

How Trees Talk to Each Other
TED
Published on Aug 30, 2016
https://www.youtube.com/watch?v=Un2yBgIAxYs&t=600s

Julia Butterfly Hill ~ Adventures in Tree Sitting
michaelofthemountain
Published on Jan 9, 2009
https://www.youtube.com/watch?v=FyLiOnmBZLw

Singing Plants at Damanhur
Bruce Starr
Published on Oct 24, 2011
https://www.youtube.com/watch?v=aZaokNmQ4eY

The Way Forest Looks From the Sky
un Ordinary
Published on Apr 19, 2019
https://www.youtube.com/watch?v=t_lfJu3r6ew

Blooming Flowers, Amazing Nature
Johnny Jabbour
Published on Jan 22, 2014
Moving Art by Louie Schwartzberg
https://www.youtube.com/watch?v=xW_AsV7k42o

The Science of Grounding
barefootwheels
Big Picture Ranch ~ downtoearthdocumentary.com
Published on Dec 16, 2017
https://www.youtube.com/watch?v=7qn_YnLudgg

Koko the Gorilla is the Voice of Nature at COP21
Noé ONG
Published on Dec 1, 2015
https://www.youtube.com/watch?v=FVuNTiqHys0

"A Good Day" with Brother David Steindle-Rast
A Network for Grateful Living
Published on Jul 10, 2007
https://www.youtube.com/watch?v=3Zl9puhwiyw&fbclid=IwAR16nE3WwIftzekMvm1IJ-NKWLdKMjsHYahwJH3yI_TYqD

"YeHa-NoHa": Wishes of Happiness and Prosperity to the Universe
AWAYTOCHANGE
Published on Jan 10, 2014
https://www.youtube.com/watch?v=QWubAMS_hc4

About the Author

DIANA LYNN KEKULE

Diana lives in the beautiful Pacific Northwest along the central Oregon coast, where she receives peace and inspiration from the sea.

Since the age of sixteen, she has been a student of metaphysical and esoteric teachings. As a seeker of personal truth, she began to engage what resonated within into a spiritual writing practice.

This path led to a reverence, kinship, and communication with the world of nature. Through the ancient indigenous ways of Earth Whisperer and shamanic healing practices, Diana continues to share her work through gatherings, seminars, and shamanic tarot.

If *Nature Speaks* did indeed speak to you,
please "Like" my Facebook page.
I encourage communication!

Follow me on Facebook: *EarthLight*
Website: *https://luvsea33.wixsite.com/earthlight*

Nature Speaks ~ A Journey to Yourself

www.ingramcontent.com/pod-product-compliance
Lightning Source LLC
Chambersburg PA
CBHW040107100526
44584CB00029BA/3819